Swimming with Krishna

Teaching Stories from the Kripalu Yoga Tradition

Edited and Commentary by

Richard Faulds

Peaceable Kingdom Books
Greenville, Virginia

ISBN: 978-0-9744106-5-4

Additional copies of this book, and other titles by Richard and Danna Faulds, are available by mail.
Send $14.00 (includes postage) to
Danna Faulds
53 Penny Lane
Greenville VA 24440
yogapoems@aol.com

Printed in the U.S.A. by
Morris Publishing®
3212 East Highway 30
Kearney, NE 68847
1-800-650-7888

This book is dedicated to Mataji Desai, a yogini held in the highest esteem by everyone in the Kripalu tradition. None who witnessed Mataji's service to her guru, Swami Kripalu, during his four year stay in America will ever forget the one pointed focus and devotion she brought to bear on every task. Few are aware of the lifetime commitment to sadhana that Mataji made upon Swami Kripalu's death in 1981, which she honored until the time of her passing in July, 2006. Bless you, Mataji, for the example of a life lived humbly and impeccably.

Special thanks to Danna Faulds, whose sensitive touch, penetrating insight, and artistic flair is reflected on every page.

Also by Danna and Richard Faulds

Go In and In: Poems From the Heart of Yoga
by Danna Faulds (Peaceable Kingdom Books 2002)

One Soul: More Poems From the Heart of Yoga
by Danna Faulds (Peaceable Kingdom Books 2003)

Prayers to the Infinite: Yoga Poems
by Danna Faulds (Peaceable Kingdom Books 2004)

From Root to Bloom, Poems and Other Writing
by Danna Faulds (Peaceable Kingdom Books 2006)

Sayings of Swami Kripalu: Inspiring Quotes from a
Contemporary Yoga Master, edited by Richard Faulds
(Peaceable Kingdom Books 2004)

Kripalu Yoga: A Guide to Practice On and Off the Mat
by Richard Faulds (Bantam Books 2005)

Lineage

Lineage is a line through time
connecting potent symbols
of the past with present practice.

Heritage gives us riverbanks
that contain energy, rules to follow
then toss aside, boundaries to
break through, and finally
the discernment to find truth
wherever it might hide.

Lineage is only as alive as those
who walk its paths just long
enough to grow strong, but not
so long that dogma becomes
a closed casket, or belief resists
officiating at its own funeral.

Danna Faulds

Table of Contents

Introduction

The moment a speaker begins spouting facts and figures, the audience is on its way to snoring. But storytelling is an altogether different affair. Ears perk up when characters are introduced. As the plot emerges, we sit on the edge of our seats, listening for nuances of circumstance and symbolism.

A compelling story engages our imagination. As images arise within us, words cease to be the primary vehicle for communication. This is the magic of a good story, which transmits the experience of "being there" in addition to exchanging information.

Down through history, parents and elders have recounted legends linking listeners to the past. Fables and folk tales did more than entertain the young, they taught values by presenting situations in which the outcome of wise and unwise actions could be seen and felt. Myths addressed deeper issues, providing perspective and guidance in complex matters such as growing into adulthood, finding and relating to a mate, living in harmony with nature, and facing death.

Taken together, these stories helped not only individuals but whole societies find meaning in the midst of life's challenges. Passed down from generation to generation, they preserved the collective wisdom we call culture, a wisdom that has supported human life, built civilizations, and informed religions over the millennia.

Spiritual teachers have also been storytellers, using myths and parables to kindle inspiration, paint a picture of humankind's place in the cosmos, and convey esoteric teachings. In our time, Joseph Campbell was a potent and powerful voice for the

9

importance of myth, stories he felt were encoded with clues to help individuals discover and make their way along the spiritual path.

Campbell and many other influential thinkers believe the world's wisdom traditions are written in a universal language of symbols and archetypes that speaks directly to the deeper mind and soul. The power of this sacred literature is available to anyone who can step beyond the literal meaning of the words to read the myth as a symbolic story, rather than a factual account of historical events. Seen in this light, the primary purpose of myth is to convey meaning and significance, not simply facts. It is this symbolic reading that allows us to discern the keys that unlock the stories.

This is not to say mythic stories are not grounded in actual events. Scholarship confirms that the names, events, and circumstances described in many myths are in accord with the historical record. While the focus of this book is not historical or academic, each chapter includes a short section linking the story to generally accepted knowledge. For those who want to know more, there is no better source that Georg Feuerstein's masterpiece *The Yoga Tradition* (Hohm Press 1998).

When read symbolically, myths have an amazing capacity to speak to individuals at different levels of development, delivering the precise message needed to catalyze positive movement. This is what makes storytelling such a powerful medium for spiritual teaching, because the meaning of a story grows with us, becoming increasingly whole and clear as we progress along the path in understanding.

Prior works on the Kripalu tradition have recounted its legends as entirely factual in nature. At the heart of these tales is Lakulish, the immortal yogi who attained a "divine body" and appears as needed to guide deserving seekers and keep the tradition potent. Possessing all the psychic powers mentioned in the yogic scriptures, Lakulish is a wonder worker whose miraculous acts are always fascinating and instructive. I honor this literal view, most fully expressed in Swami Rajarshi Muni's *Infinite Grace, the Story of My Spiritual Lineage* (Life Mission Publications 2002).

At the same time, the tales of Lakulish and others can be read as deeply symbolic. Interpreted in this light, these teaching stories convey vital messages for anyone treading the Kripalu Yoga path. That is how they have spoken to me, and it is that perspective that I aim to investigate here.

Swami Kripalu told many stories. Most were simple, uplifting tales to illustrate his public discourses, keep the audience alert, and generate a good laugh. Other stories were of a different nature, more compelling and often not fully explained.

In reflecting on this second type of story, I have come to believe they are like pieces of a puzzle that fit together to form an elegant whole. It is these stories that are presented in this volume, along with my thoughts about their significance. My hope is that they may inform your yoga practice and life in positive ways, as they have mine.

Now on to the stories!

Richard Faulds
Greenville, Virginia

Chapter One

Practice, Practice, Practice

The Kripalu Yoga tradition reaches back five thousand years to an ascetic named Vishvamitra, who practiced a precursor to yoga called *tapas*. *Tapas* means to *generate heat and light,* a reference to the psychic heat and spiritual radiance generated by the practice of austerities like fasting and celibacy. Through prolonged tapas, ascetics like Vishvamitra strengthened their willpower and sought to accumulate psychic power, win the favor of the gods, and attain divine boons. While engaged in this process, they pioneered the psychospiritual techniques that developed into what we know as yoga.

The Legend of Vishvamitra's Tapas

Before embarking on the path of tapas, Vishvamitra was a king named Kaushika who ruled his subjects well. As was the custom of his day, Kaushika and his army would travel throughout the kingdom to assure the safety of his subjects. Kaushika honored the rules that applied to his station in life, and one such rule was that a king should not pass the hermitage of a sage or holy person without stopping to pay respects and ask for his or her blessing. In return, the sage would welcome the king and offer him food and hospitality. Such was the order of things.

One day Kaushika was passing by the hermitage of a Brahmin holy man named Vashishtha. Kaushika could see a stream wending its way through grounds full of flowering trees and shrubs. Deer and other animals walked freely about, and the air resounded with the music of birds. Coming nearer, the king noticed sages bent on performing tapas, and others lost in meditation. An aura of peace permeated the atmosphere.

13

It seemed to Kaushika that the realm of the gods was not in the sky, as he had been taught, but right here in Vashishtha's hermitage.

Kaushika entered and bowed low before the sage. Vashishtha welcomed him with warmth and fanfare, sending for a seat befitting a king and making Kaushika sit upon it like a throne. He offered the king fruits and milk, which Kaushika received with reverence and humility. Then they spoke of general things. Vashishtha asked, "I hope your family is well, and that your subjects are happy under your rule, which I am sure is righteous. Are your servants honest and obedient? Is your army large and powerful? Are your enemies subdued? Is your treasury full?"

Kaushika answered in the affirmative, and in turn inquired about the health of the sage, if the residents of his hermitage were able to pursue their tapas without disturbance from bandits or wild animals, and if they lacked for any material goods. Each had respect for the other, and in the midst of these formalities a genuine affection sprung up between them.

After they had talked about many things, Vashishtha said, "You are a righteous king and a good man, and I would like to entertain you and your army this evening." Kaushika imagined the simple sage was unaware of the number and appetite of his soldiers. To save Vashishtha from embarrassment, he said, "Your words, full of affection, have touched me deeply. You have given me food and drink, and basking in your presence has renewed my spirit. I will soon be taking leave of you to continue my journey." Kaushika rose up tactfully as if to go, but Vashishtha persisted until courtesy required him to accept the sage's hospitality.

Unbeknownst to Kaushika, Vashishtha had come into possession of a wish-fulfilling cow named Surabhi through his tapas. With a mere swish of her tail, all preparations were made. When the army arrived at the hermitage, each man was entertained in a manner that exceeded the luxury granted Kaushika in his royal court. Kaushika was told of the magical cow and saw she had a lovely shape, a gleaming coat of mottled color, and eyes that were soft and gentle.

Coveting the cow, Kaushika interrupted the gaiety to address all those present, "My lord, never in my life have I tasted food like this eaten by us this night. I am greatly impressed by the power of your cow and want to ask a favor of you. Such a cow should be possessed by the king of a country so her bounty can benefit everyone. Please give her to me, and I will give you a thousand cows."

Vashishtha was taken aback by the words of Kaushika. But he composed himself and softly said, "I hate to refuse anyone anything. But not even for a hundred thousand or a thousand thousand cows will I give up my Surabhi. She is part of me, and cannot be separated from me. I have no use for wealth in any form that you could offer. My answer is no, and that is certain."

Kaushika was stunned. Never before had a desire of his been frustrated. Anger took possession of Kaushika, who ordered his soldiers to seize the cow. With a shake of her body, hundreds of warriors appeared that easily defeated Kaushika's forces. Kaushika's sons entered the fray, quickly thinning out the ranks of the opposing warriors, but the cow just created more. Then Kaushika ordered his sons to attack Vashishtha, who raised his staff and burned every one of them to ash.

The king was heartbroken. His army was destroyed and his sons were dead. Like a serpent with its fangs pulled out, like a bird whose wings have been clipped, he was vanquished and humiliated.

Kaushika relinquished his throne and retired to the northern forests to perform tapas. He went without food, water, or companionship. He refrained from lying down and sleeping. In the summer, Kaushika sat in the center of a circle of five fires. In the winter, he sat naked in the snow. Kaushika's thoughts were always hovering around the humiliating defeat he had suffered at the hands of Vashishtha. Inwardly, Kaushika called again and again upon Lord Shiva to appear and grant him a boon.

Many years passed, and the power of Kaushika's tapas grew so great that the ground began to tremble. Mountains spit fire and the seas lashed their waves. Fearing for the welfare of the earth, the gods gathered and begged Shiva to grant Kaushika's wish and end his austerities. Appearing before Kaushika, Shiva inquired, "Why are you performing this tapas? What do you desire?" Kaushika prostrated and sang Shiva's praises. He then asked to be made supremely proficient in the art of archery and granted every spiritual power useful in combat. Shiva said, "I have given them to you, now go in peace."

Kaushika's pride was restored, and he said to himself, "Vashishtha the great is as good as dead. I will destroy him and bring that cow to my kingdom." Kaushika proceeded directly to Vashishtha's hermitage. Arriving, he raised his bow and let fly a flurry of arrows and the incantations that rendered them powerful. The hermitage was quickly destroyed, its residents fleeing in fear, and even the soil beneath it left bare, salty and fit for nothing.

His staff glowing red hot, Vashishtha came before Kaushika and said, "This peaceful hermitage is ruined, and I am very angry with you." Kaushika had lived this moment many times in his mind and was not afraid. Relishing his revenge, Kaushika loosed his full arsenal against his hated foe. Amazingly, Vashishtha was able to deflect all Kaushika's weapons simply by raising his staff.

Vashishtha then cursed Kaushika, saying, "You are a disgrace to the warrior caste. Acknowledge the divine power of the Brahmins." Kaushika threw down his bow and exclaimed, "Fie on the power of a warrior. The only power worth having is that of a Brahmin." Inwardly, he vowed to perform tapas until he too became a Brahmin.

Kaushika's hatred for Vashishtha was now immense. He traveled to the southern forests determined to conduct the most demanding tapas. He stood on one foot, never slept, and took air as his only food. It is said that Kaushika's tapas was so intense that wisps of smoke could be seen wafting out of his ears.

After a thousand years, Kaushika was glowing like the sun itself, and the earth was in danger of being burned up. In heaven, the rising temperatures were upsetting the wives of the gods, whose complaining became intolerable. Indra's throne became too hot to sit upon. In desperation, Indra summoned Menaka, the finest woman in his court, and said, "Kaushika is performing tapas and glowing like the noonday sun. Go to him. With your beauty and winning ways, make him succumb to the weakness in the heart of every man. If he abandons his tapas, I will be pleased with you."

Menaka was afraid and said, "Lord, I have been told Kaushika is very powerful and quick tempered. Think of this

17

combination: anger and tapas. You yourself are afraid of him, yet you want me to face him." Despite these concerns, Indra persuaded her to go. Menaka went down to earth and spent several years in the vicinity of Kaushika, waiting for the proper moment to make her appearance.

One day Kaushika got up from meditation and was moving about. Menaka walked by the spot with her eyes looking away from him. Just as he noticed her, a faint breeze blew her shawl aside, revealing her heavenly form. Then she slowly turned her lovely face towards him.

Five years passed, and another five, before Kaushika awoke from this pleasurable dream and remembered his tapas. At first he was angry with himself, but slowly it dawned on him that this was the work of the gods set out to disturb him. Menaka, holding their daughter in her arms, could see what was transpiring on his face. She was overcome with fear, but Kaushika was not angry with her.

Bidding Menaka farewell, Kaushika said he was simply continuing where he had left off. Kaushika traveled west and his tapas was terrible. He held both arms aloft and never closed his eyes. Years passed, and once again the gods found themselves concocting ways to distract Kaushika.

It came to pass that a disciple of Vashishtha named Trishanku asked his guru for an unusual boon: to be admitted into heaven in his mortal body. Vashishtha denied his request, saying that it was an impious and improper wish. Unsatisfied by his guru's response, Trishanku approached Kaushika, who seized upon this opportunity to outdo and embarrass Vashishtha.

Kaushika peformed a ritual that called upon the gods and requested them to gather. When all the rulers of heaven were present and listening, Kaushika asked them to accept Trishanku into heaven. Seeing an opportunity to exhaust his storehouse of tapas, the gods insulted Kaushika and refused his request. Ignoring their refusal, Kaushika raised Trishanku into the sky with the force of his tapas. A tug of war ensued between the gods and Kaushika, in which Trishanku see-sawed between heaven and earth.

In the end, Kaushika was able to grant Trishanku's request by creating a whole new universe, ruled over by another set of gods, who were willing to accept him into their heaven. Although Kaushika was victorious, his treasury of tapas was once again empty.

Kaushika traveled east and found a secluded spot. He observed total silence, refused to eat or drink, and even his consumption of air was regulated. After some number of years, Indra grew concerned that Kaushika was going to usurp his status as the most powerful being in the universe. Another of his heavenly courtesans was sent, but Kaushika recognized the ploy. Turning her to stone with a curse, Kaushika realized in the next moment that this display of anger was yet another lapse from his tapas, which he resumed immediately.

Breathing regularly, Kaushika's mind gradually grew peaceful. After spending many years lost in trance, Kaushika was awakened by a young boy crying in his lap. As Kaushika opened his eyes, the boy said, "I have no father, no mother, and no kinsmen. I have been told you are very powerful and very compassionate. You are my only refuge. Please help me." Pacifying the boy, Kaushika learned that he was the middle of three sons. The father preferred the eldest, the mother was fond of the youngest, and he had been sold for a few cows to be the subject of a human sacrifice.

Kaushika told the boy, "Go and allow yourself to be tied to the sacrificial post. They will place garlands around your neck and smear sandalwood paste on your body. At that time, begin repeating in your mind this two verse hymn. When the ceremony is at its zenith, sing it out loud." The boy learned the hymn with great care and left Kaushika grateful and confident.

Doing as he was told, the sacrificial chamber fell silent when the boy's words rang out, at first with surprise and then with admiration for the nobility of his hymn, which eloquently praised the gods. Empowered by Kaushika's tapas, the hymn caused the gods to appear in person, grant the wishes of those conducting the sacrifice, and bless the boy with long life and good fortune.

Although he acted out of compassion, Kaushika's treasury of tapas had once again been diminished. Hearing of the boy's success, he returned to his trance for a thousand more years, steadily deepening his concentration. About this time, the Gayatri mantra was revealed to Kaushika, and his practice shifted from tapas to one of the earliest forms of yoga, mantra meditation. Inwardly, Kaushika intoned the prayer to a measured and melodic meter:

Almighty God! Thou art the giver of life, the remover of pain and sorrow, and the bestower of happiness. Creator of the Universe, illumine my intellect with thy sin-destroying light and guide me along the path of righteousness.

Meditating on this prayer of divine origin, all obstacles fell away and Kaushika realized the Brahman. Feeling completely at peace, Kaushika noticed he was thin as a stick. He cooked some rice and prepared to break his fast of many years. Just as he was about to eat, Indra appeared before Kaushika in the form of an orange clad mendicant begging for food. Kaushika spoke not a word but happily handed him all the rice.

Seeing that Kaushika looked upon the beggar's hunger as no different from his own, Brahma appeared to Kaushika, and said, "With your own efforts, you have achieved the status of a Brahmin. May you prosper." Kaushika prostrated before Brahma and spoke, "If what you say is true, the great sage Vashishtha should recognize me as such." Vashishtha came forth saying, "There is no doubt about it. You are a great man and a Brahmin." A thin smile lit up the face of Kaushika, who honored Vashishtha with true affection. Because the foremost thought in his mind was to do good to others, he was given the name Vishvamitra which means "friend of the universe."

Vishvamitra wandered until he discovered a suitable location to establish a place of pilgrimage. Through the power of his tapas, he altered the course of the holy Ganges in the north, connecting it with the Rangavati river, which flowed nearby. Using this now holy source of water, he created several deep pools for pilgrims to bathe. The site was completed with the building of the Brahmeshvar temple, which housed a black Shiva lingam made of meteorite. The pilgrimage place came to be known as "Medhavati," which means "place of purified intellect." It was from here that Vishvamitra propagated the practice of tapas, Shiva worship, and mantra yoga.

News of Vishvamitra spread far and wide. With characteristic zeal, Vishvamitra resumed his tapas, intent on making his pilgrimage site the most famous in all India, surpassing even Kashi in its glory. Shortly thereafter, Vishnu appeared in the form of an old, deaf holy man. Distracting Vishvamitra from his tapas, Vishnu revealed his true form and said, "Great Brahmin, your efforts are not in vain. This pilgrimage site will be an important seat of learning. Those who inhabit this place will quickly become pure of heart and the holy Gayatri mantra will resound throughout the universe. Yet it will not compete with Kashi."

On hearing this, Vishvamitra became despondent. Vishnu empathized, saying, "Do not be disheartened. Your dream will be fulfilled when Shiva himself incarnates in this place." Vishvamitra accepted the divine plan. Living a long life, he inspired many to pursue the path of tapas and yoga. Emanating from Medhavati and other places of pilgrimage and learning, the Vedic culture of India spread throughout the land and remained vital for several thousand years.

Commentary

The story of Vishvamitra's life colorfully conveys the transformative power of self-discipline. Ancient India was a highly structured society built upon a rigid caste system. Although Kaushika was a warrior king, the superiority of the priestly Brahmins – a word meaning born from the mouth of God – was taken for granted. In the context of his time, the assertion that a person could raise himself up to the spiritual status of a Brahmin through personal effort was radical and revolutionary. This story tells us that we all have untapped potential lying dormant within us, hidden capacities that can be awakened through what Kripalu Yoga calls "willful practice."

At the beginning of the story, Kaushika is depicted as a virtuous and dutiful king, which signifies his fitness to embark on the spiritual path. As is often the case, Kaushika's point of entry comes through contact with a spiritual teacher. Vashishtha's enlightened state is symbolized by his wish-fulfilling cow, which has satisfied all his desires and "is part of him and cannot be separated from him."

While there is mutual respect and genuine warmth between the two men at the outset, Kaushika's relationship with Vashishtha quickly turns into a profound and long lasting struggle. Vashishtha's choice to refrain from simply killing Kaushika suggests the sage is aware that Kaushika has the capacity to make the shift from king to enlightened sage. Vashishtha's dinner invitation might even have been intended to set this whole chain of events into motion. Consciously or unconsciously, spiritual teachers like Vashishtha often fulfill their role in unusual ways.

Kaushika sets out upon the path of tapas with a truly base motive: revenge. This may seem odd, but in truth everyone embarks on the spiritual path for the wrong reasons. Unconsciously, we want to be loved, find relief from suffering, attain power over others, or simply avoid the rigors of facing life directly and honestly. It is only by walking the path, and wandering repeatedly off it, that our motivations are slowly but surely purified.

Although we may have an intuitive sense of our hidden potential, few embark on the path without considerable baggage and a multiplicity of wrong views. It could be said that the main purpose of spiritual practice is to purify us of whatever notions are holding us back. At the outset Kaushika views tapas as a path to vanquish his nemesis and fulfill his egocentric needs and desires. As he journeys onward, this view is turned on its head, with Kaushika being repeatedly humbled. Realization comes only when he is able to let go of his quest for power and status, and sincerely surrender to a higher power.

The duration and intensity of Kaushika's tapas graphically describe the challenge inherent in the spiritual journey, which involves the interruption of innumerable ingrained habits and self-serving patterns of behavior. As the fire of transformation

23

blazes, internal energies build to the breaking point and external situations invariably arise to distract the aspirant from going forward. Instead of being immune to distraction, Kaushika succumbs to every temptation that tests him. Despite falling prey to greed, anger, lust, pride, and sentimentality, Kaushika sooner or later remembers his intention and resumes his tapas. These "lapses" are actually the learning process in action, which is the meaning behind the Kripalu Yoga credo, "practice, practice, practice."

While each of us is spurred on by an inner urge to grow, there is a definite cost to speeding up the pace of our evolution. The homeostasis of our life is disturbed, time and time again, as the fire of transformation rages. Kaushika's tapas keeps all the gods on edge, disrupting them from enjoying heaven, symbolizing the socially acceptable pleasures we all use to dull and distract ourselves.

This story is a clear warning that the spiritual path is demanding. Tapas is done in all four directions, reflecting a need to uplift every area of our lives, and all three Hindu deities – Shiva, Brahma and Vishnu – are eventually encountered. No stone is left unturned on the road to realization.

As his lower nature is brought into balance, Kaushika is able to make a crucial shift. His tapas of inner struggle ceases, and he lets go of external austerities like sitting near fires and holding his arms aloft. There is a beautiful "story within a story" about the boy sold for sacrifice. As mortals awaiting death, each of us shares his predicament. Looked at in this light, the best we can do is go willingly, singing life's praises

As Kaushika starts to regulate the flow of his breath, he has commenced the practice of pranayama so integral to yoga. As

24

a result, Kaushika falls first into trance and then into peaceful meditation. Instead of thoughts hovering around hatred and desire, a prayer of reverent worship arises within him. With this as his focal point, Kaushika is able to dive deep and realize the Brahman. Returning from trance, he is a truly a changed person, his personality and character indelibly stamped by what was traditionally called the Brahmavidya – supreme knowledge of the Absolute.

Kaushika's realization does not go untested. Indra appears in a guise strikingly similar to Vashishtha to eat his rice. This is to ensure that Kaushika has woven the truth of spiritual oneness into the very fabric of his being. Life is full of rice eaters and other aggravations that test our mettle. In the Kripalu tradition, it is not the power of a yoga experience, but its expression in daily life that is the true measure of enlightenment. Kaushika is pronounced a Brahmin only after he treats the hunger of another as equivalent to his own.

Kaushika is given the name Vishvamitra to signify his unconditional positive regard for all beings. If there is any guidance that can be trusted to hold true at any stage of the Kripalu Yoga path, it is this inward stance of being the well wisher of self and others.

After realization, it is noteworthy that Vishvamitra remains to some extent his stubborn and ornery self, embarking to make his pilgrimage spot the best of any in India. Yet when Vishnu appears to say this is not in the cards, Vishvamitra is able to let go without a fight.

Vishvamitra goes on to promote a path in which adherents learn to restrain the wayward mind and senses through austerities; internalize awareness through pranayama and mantra meditation; and awaken to the vast ocean of being that underlies the individual waves of bodymind and personality.

The goal of this ascetic path is symbolized in the Shiva lingam installed as the focus of worship in the Brahmeshvar temple. The lingam represents the Absolute, eternal and unchanging dimension of reality as contrasted against the constant flux of the relative and time-bound world, the detached male principle as opposed to the embodied feminine. Asceticism almost always involves a rejection of the physical in order to realize the spiritual, and that is the case here.

The story ends with a hint that there is more to come. While self-discipline can bring many things, the highest is beyond its reach.

History

Scholars believe Vishvamitra lived circa 3500 B.C.E. Along with Vashishtha, Vishvamitra is remembered as one of seven great rishis – a word meaning seer – whose collective wisdom established the Vedic culture we know as Hinduism. Of the seven, Vishvamitra was the only one not born a Brahmin. The full story of Vishvamitra's tapas can be found in the *Srimad Bhagavatam*.

The Gayatri mantra is one of India's most sacred prayers. It appears in the Rig Veda, the oldest book in humankind's library, written circa 3000 B.C.E., and is still recited each morning by pious Hindus. For a quality soundtrack of the Gayatri Mantra by a contemporary Kripalu chanter and teacher, see *Soul Flight: Chanted Mantras for Healing and Illumination* by Bhavani Lorraine Nelson.

Although a forerunner of yoga, tapas continued to be practiced as an independent tradition long after the birth of yoga. For more on the history of tapas and the fascinating feats of its great *tapasvins*, see *The Yoga Tradition* by Georg Feuerstein.

As one of the *five prescribed observances* or *niyama* universally embraced by the yoga tradition, tapas remains a vital element of contemporary yoga practice.

In *Premyatra, Pilgrimage of Love,* Swami Kripalu taught the essential principles of yogic tapas as follows: "The meaning of the term *tapas* is profound. To equate it with simple austerity is not proper. Yet this is the ordinary understanding where we must begin. Just as energy can be produced by damming a river, one can generate energy by practicing tapas using countless yogic techniques. It can be said that a seeker only progresses to the extent that the three-fold tapas of body, mind, and speech is accomplished, for it is through tapas that purification takes place. If one begins by attempting to accomplish tapas of the body, tapas of speech and mind will automatically follow. Tapas is much like the process of smelting fine metals. As fire purifies gold, restraint and spiritual disciplines purify the seeker."

Chapter Two

Born Divine

The central figure in the Kripalu Yoga tradition is a mysterious yoga adept named Lakulish. Lakulish is the twenty-eight and most recent incarnation of Shiva, the Hindu deity closely associated with yoga and the quest for self-transformation. Images of Lakulish appear in temples all over India, and archeologists have unearthed coins bearing his likeness, but little is known about Lakulish's life beyond the legend of his miraculous birth and death.

The story opens with a reference back to the Vedic culture established by Vishvamitra and other rishis thousands of years ago. Having grown stagnant for want of potent teachers, it is sorely in need of revival.

The Life of Lakulish

Lakulish was born in the village that sprang up around Medhavati, the pilgrimage site established by Vishvamitra. His father's name was Vishvarup and his mother was Sudharshana. Descended from a long ancestral line of Brahmins, the life of their household orbited around a schedule of ceremonies, rituals and other sacred rites.

Shortly after Sudarshana gave birth to a son, Vishvarup prepared to go on a lengthy pilgrimage. Traveling on foot to visit holy places, his intent was to ask the gods to bestow good qualities upon the boy. Before departing, he instructed Sudharshana to continue the family's religious observances in his absence. She was to prepare the necessary materials each morning, and seek the help of a local priest to perform the ceremonies later in the day.

After three months, a strange event began to occur. Sudharshana would leave the house to fetch the priest and return home to find the elaborate ceremony performed. The sacred fire would be lit, and all the ceremonial articles bearing signs that evidenced their proper use. Yet the house was empty except for the infant child sleeping in the cradle. This did not happen once. It happened on the second, third, and fourth days too. Then it became a daily occurrence and neither Sudarshana nor the priest could explain it.

When Vishvarup returned, Sudarshana recounted the whole story. Determined to solve the mystery, Vishvarup concealed himself in an adjacent house. While hiding, he was amazed to see his infant son climb out of his crib, carry out the ceremony with perfection, and then crawl back into his bed.

Amazed and overjoyed, Vishvarup and Sudarshana entered the house and hugged their son. Knowing these capacities heralded the birth of a most unusual child, Vishvarup inquired, "Son, tell us who you really are?" The child instantly fainted, and his body became lifeless. All efforts to revive the boy proved futile, and the mood of Vishvarup and Sudarshana shifted from joy to grief.

As was the custom of the time, Vishvarup and Sudarshana laid the child's body to rest in a nearby pond. The unusual events continued, as tortoises appeared to carry the body into the pond's depths, placing it at the base of a Shiva lingam installed there by local holy men. A few months passed, and Vishvarup and Sudarshana returned to their lives, attempting to make sense of what had happened and not lose themselves in sorrow and grief.

Meanwhile and unbeknownst to anyone, the infant's body was undergoing a profound metamorphosis. Growing quickly into a youth, the boy floated to the surface and was found by the local sages playing on the surface of the water with a stick in his hand. Seeing his radiant countenance, the sages asked, "Who are you?"

The boy answered: "I am prana." The sages were intrigued by this response, prana being a yogic term. Engaging the boy in dialogue, the sages were amazed at his penetrating wisdom. He was called Lakulish (club carrier) because he held a stick in his hand when he was discovered. Ascertaining his complete mastery of yoga, they determined he was the incarnation of Shiva foretold by Vishnu long ago.

News of the incarnation spread. Sages, royalty, and seekers from far-off places began arriving to receive Lakulish's audience. The name of the village was changed to Kayavarohan, which means "Shiva descended into a human body." With Lakulish in residence, the rural pilgrimage site quickly grew into a flourishing city, renowned for the purity and prosperity of its inhabitants. Under Lakulish's guidance, many aspirants became realized yoga masters and powerful teachers. Lakulish directed them to locate throughout the land and rejuvenate India's spiritual culture.

After many years, Lakulish summoned his principle disciples to Kayavaron, asking them to gather at an appointed hour in the Brahmeshvar temple. Everyone was puzzled by the same question: "Why has Lakulish called us together?" A host of disciples, kings, ascetics, and devotees also arrived to participate. Seated up front near the Shiva lingam installed by Vishvamitra ages ago, Lakulish announced, "My life mission has been fulfilled, and my time on earth is drawing to a close. I want to say goodbye before merging into the infinite."

Overcome with despair, the throng broke into wails of anguish. Lakulish's chief disciples performed a ceremony honoring their guru. Afterwards, Lakulish gave everyone his most auspicious blessing, and instructed the group, "Close your eyes for a moment of silent prayer."

Falling instantly into profound meditation, the gathering came out its collective reverie to find that Lakulish had merged into the lingam. Devotees believe that Shiva, in the form of Lakulish, is to this day seated in the Brahmeshvar temple at Kayavarohan.

Commentary

The key that unlocks this story is understanding that Lakulish represents a second stage in the Kripalu path, a way to realize the deeper spirituality hinted at near the end of the Vishvamitra story.

In the same way that Jesus comes only after John the Baptist has preached repentance, Lakulish comes only after the message of Vishvamitra has inspired a seeker to heal, strengthen, and purify the bodymind through a regimen of willful practice. Until one has cleaned up his lifestyle and sincerely wrestled with his shortcomings, the teachings conveyed by this story remain inapplicable. The seeds of spiritual awakening can only sprout when the soil of body and mind has been properly tilled.

The infant boy, already proficient in ceremonial worship, represents a mature individual, someone with the devotional bent and steady mind required to conduct complex rituals. With these capacities developed, the focus of practice can shift to a profound exploration of the sense of self.

This exploration of identity is most evident in the Vedantic technique of self-inquiry, which uses the question "Who am I?" to drill down through the personality and into the divine root of our being. When asked directly, "Who are you?" the boy faints. Losing contact with the external world, it appears that he has died. Actually he has disappeared inside to contemplate the question, and activity is taking place in subtle realms.

The tortoises that carry away Lakulish's body symbolize the fifth stage of yoga called *pratyahar*, a word meaning *withdrawal from the senses*. Like a tortoise that can draw its limbs and head into its shell, an adept yogi can withdraw his attention from the senses to enter a state of inner absorption. With the mind introverted, profound inner work can be undertaken and accomplished.

Bodies of water are universal symbols for the psyche. Carried to the bottom of the pond and placed before the Shiva lingam, the story tells us that the boy's trance was profound and his intention in diving so deep within was to encounter the divine.

While lost to the world in meditation, the boy realizes his true identity. Although his body has not died, the death metaphor is consciously employed here to signify a death-rebirth experience as well as a deep trance. What dies is the boy's psychological identity as a spiritual seeker, worshiper, and devotee.

This is an important point, as most seekers unconsciously assume their egocentric self can be polished to the point where they "get enlightened." In actuality, awakening only occurs when the personal identity falls way, revealing the trans-personal spirit or Self. In the language of Zen, this is regaining "the original face you had before you were born," a reference to the simple and spacious presence always lying beneath the conditioned mind. When the small self dies, what remains is the divine incarnate – Shiva as Lakulish.

Emerging from the pond, the boy's transformed body floats to the surface, and he returns to consciousness. When found by the holy men, he is again asked, "Who are you?" Now able to answer the question, he proclaims, "I am prana," stating that he is a pure expression of the source energy that activates the breath, animates the body, and illumines the mind. Trace any of these visible aspects of your being back to its invisible source, and there you will discover prana, the subtle energy that radiates from the soul.

The youth is recognized by the holy men as an incarnation of Shiva. This indicates that prana is a pure emanation of divine consciousness. This is a very different message from that of Vishvamitra, who is hell-bent on controlling the flow of prana that lies beneath the habitual activity of his mind and senses.

At first Vishvamitra works to restrain his energy so he is not led astray by strong urges and feelings. Eventually he is able to channel it into worthy thoughts and actions. The legend of Lakulish suggests a next step. Once a measure of purification has been accomplished, a yogi can dive deep to realize that every level of his being originates from a divine source. A natural harmony arises and inner conflict resolves. Instead of things to thwart or control, the faculties of body, heart, and mind become trustworthy faculties to guide us in life.

Interpreted properly, this story is not anointing Lakulish as special. It is declaring that each of us is in truth born divine. At this juncture of the path, the focus of practice shifts from disciplined doing to non-doing or surrender, and one's expression in life is likely to change. Other contrasts between Vishvamitra and Lakulish are significant.

Where Vishvamitra's grinding process of purification takes forever, Lakulish's metamorphosis takes place quickly, suggesting that transformation at this stage can be rapid, occurring in quantum leaps rather than incremental steps. Vishvamitra is a hoary old anchorite, but Lakulish is young, vital, radiant, and playful. Vishvamitra lives in a remote pilgrimage site. Lakulish inhabits a city where commerce and the arts flourish. Vishvamitra glimpses deeper truths and discerns the existence of spirit. Lakulish looks more closely to discover that he is spirit incarnate, free to live an enlightened life in the world.

All this and more is symbolized in the statue Lakulish leaves behind in the temple, the body of a yogi merged with the infinite. This statue reflects the teachings of Tantra, which consider absolute and relative, masculine and feminine, and all opposites as two aspects of an indivisible whole. By viewing every facet of life as a divine expression, Tantra shatters the rigid distinction between worldly and spiritual that undergirds most forms of yoga relying exclusively on self-discipline.

History

Scholars believe Lakulish lived in central India circa 200 C.E. A contemporary of Patanjali, the author of the Yoga Sutra, Lakulish authored the lesser known Pashupat Sutra, a text that has proven difficult to meaningfully translate. Like other esoteric works, the Pashupat Sutra is written in a secret language called *sandha bhasha* (twilight language) that relies upon the use of symbolic terms only decipherable to initiates. This approach was taken to protect the teachings of the tradition from degradation, and also to prevent uninitiated individuals from dabbling in its powerful practices.

While established in the second century, the Pashupats are part of the oldest known yoga tradition. This tradition traces itself back through 27 prior incarnations of Shiva, with a famous piece of archeological evidence called the "Pashupat seal" dating back to 3000 B.C.E. found in the ruins of Harappa and Mohenjo Daro.

The Pashupats were a staunch religious sect whose teachings proclaim that a unitary force and consciousness underlies creation and indwells our being. Relating to this force as a supreme being, they called it *Shiva* which means *benign* or *auspicious*. This spiritual force remains hidden to most of us, who mistakenly identify with the constant flux of body and mind, versus the steady light of the eternal soul. This pivotal mistake causes the light of the soul to be obscured by the animal drives and desires (pashu) that dominate the psyche.

The Pashupats were one of many groups who developed the techniques of kundalini yoga, through which they believed that aspirants can master their animal nature and become "pashu-pati." Becoming a yoga adept was a necessary first step toward liberation, which was seen as a union of the self (*jiva*) with the Lord (*Shiva*) that occurs only through surrender and grace. A liberated being lives as a *jivan mukti*, a soul fully awake in the body whose actions are constantly informed by the divine. Swami Kripalu considered himself a pilgrim on this Pashupat kundalini yoga path.

Although expressed quite differently, the teachings of Kripalu Yoga are in accord with those of the Pashupats. The first step is to heal and harmonize the whole being through basic yoga practices and healthy lifestyle. The aim here is to build vitality and gain proficiency in life. The second step is to awaken energy through deeper practices, gradually purifying body, heart and mind. The third step is to surrender to free flowing energy and intuitive awareness, both on the yoga mat and in life, cultivating a living relationship with spirit.

Swami Kripalu first visited Kayavorahan in 1955 after being asked to speak during a holy week of celebrations sponsored by the village. Living in seclusion and focused on his yoga practice, Swami Kripalu routinely received and refused such requests. Yet for some reason, he agreed to speak.

Touring the village, the local elders proudly showed Swami Kripalu a stone lingam found in a farmer's field. This statue was markedly different from the hundreds of other red sandstone carvings found nearby in various states of decomposition. Made of meteorite, its black surface was perfectly smooth despite its antiquity.

Seeing the statue, Swami Kripalu felt faint and had to hold the wall for support. It was a perfect representation of a yogi who had appeared to Swami Kripalu at several pivotal moments of his adult life to offer guidance and support. He believed that this divine yogi was none other than his guru's "true form," whose history Swami Kripalu was told he would one day discover.

That evening, Swami Kripalu saw a vision of Kayavarohan's former splendor during meditation and felt he was given a divine command to rebuild the Brahmeshvar temple so it could once again house the ancient statue. Although a penniless monk, Swami Kripalu undertook this project. Writing and speaking about the cultural and spiritual importance of Kayavarohan, Swami Kripalu raised the funds and oversaw the rebuilding of the temple, which was completed in 1974.

Chapter Three

Swept Across the Threshold

Instead of a mythic figure of ages past, the next story involves a contemporary yogi who can be introduced with a fair degree of certainty as to the circumstances of his life.

Swami Kripalu was born into a cultured Brahmin family in 1913. The family was native to Dabhoi, a town of modest size in the state of Gujarat. At the age of seven, Swami Kripalu's father died, plunging the large family of seven daughters and two sons into financial hardship. Although plagued by the difficulties that accompany extreme poverty, Swami Kripalu's family remained loving and close.

The family's debt steadily increased until their home was foreclosed upon by creditors, and their scant possessions put out on the street. To contribute to the support of his mother and sisters, the young Swami Kripalu left school at 14 and worked a series of low paying jobs in Dabhoi. Turning 18, he left to join his elder brother in the metropolis of Bombay, where he hoped to find steady employment and help save his family from its financial crisis.

It was at this time that Swami Kripalu encountered a nameless and mysterious guru. Invited to visit his prosperous ashram, Swami Kripalu was received as the guru's foremost disciple and affectionately referred to as "Swami." Over a period of 15 months, he was schooled in the scriptures, taught the rudiments of yoga, and guided through a 108 day purification regimen that ended with a 40-day water fast. Told he was destined to commence practice and become a yoga adept later in life, the youth was seemingly abandoned by his guru.

Living as a bachelor for a decade, Swami Kripalu supported himself as a music teacher and playwright. Narrowly escaping an effort by his family to arrange marriage, he was initiated into the religious order of swamis at 29. Given the name Kripalu, he spent nine years traveling about the state of Gujarat on foot, clad in saffron robes, and carrying a begging bowl.

Moving from village to village, Swami Kripalu's talents as a musician, singer, and speaker turned many hearts to God. Wealthy individuals saw his purity and gave him sizeable donations, enabling Swami Kripalu to establish temples, libraries and schools in villages throughout western India. Always using the funds to help those in need, Swami Kripalu continued to live simply and in accord with his monastic vows.

At the age of 38, Swami Kripalu ceased wandering to commence an intensive practice of yoga or *sadhana*. He began with three one-hour sittings of alternate nostril pranayama each day. Regular pranayama heightened the sensitivity of Swami Kripalu's body, leading him to radically change his diet. Gradually intensifying his practice of pranayama and eating sparingly of simple foods, Swami Kripalu experienced the awakening of the life force called *pranothana* that leads to "natural" yoga. After only a few rounds of alternate nostril breathing, Swami Kripalu's mind would fall into meditation and witness his body spontaneously perform hundreds of postures and other hatha yoga techniques.

At the time of this story, Swami Kripalu was entirely absorbed in sadhana. His longing for God was intense, and the following lyrics from one of his bhajans (devotional songs), graphically conveys his inner state:

Oh Lord, I have come to your feet.
Despite having eyes, I am totally blind.
The road to the divine is unknown to me.
I am crying for help every moment.

I have always lived my life according to the scriptures.
I have traveled to every holy place of pilgrimage on earth.
I have bathed in every holy stream.
I have kindled lamps in every temple,
but still have not found my destination.

I have practiced yoga.
I have lost my sanity in devotion,
yet I am not relieved of my mind's distractions.
Oh ocean of love, grant me the inner heart's vision.

Swami Kripalu and the Narmada River

After years of disciplined practice, Swami Kripalu's progress stalled. Despite access to the rapturous states of *dharana* (concentrated awareness) and ecstatic states of *dhyana* (meditative awareness), despite the joyous heart-opening that accompanies *anahat nada* (spontaneous singing and dancing), Swami Kripalu remained frustrated in his efforts to attain *samadhi* (mystical union) and the peace that passeth all understanding.

Practicing ten hours a day in a structured lifestyle, Swami Kripalu's time in the meditation room was interspersed with breaks that promoted regularity in eating, relating with students, and sleeping. While this approach was in accord with traditional limits on the duration of spiritual practice, the drive to complete his sadhana, no matter what the cost, became irresistible and overpowering.

Tossing caution aside, Swami Kripalu began to meditate around the clock, remaining in yogic states for days at a time. Eating almost nothing, sleeping little, his sole aim was to cross the threshold into samadhi. It was at this time that Swami Kripalu developed the dark circles under his eyes that remained with him for the rest of his life.

The villagers gradually became accustomed to the uncharacteristic behavior that resulted from this change in Swami Kripalu's lifestyle. At times the normally reserved swami would wander out of his hut naked and disoriented. Tortured by the heat of an inner fire, Swami Kripalu would knock on the door of a hut or house and shout, "I am Shiva. Pour water on me." Doused with a bucketful, he would run to the next house, and then the next, to obtain some relief.

Such divine intoxication was a known phenomenon in Indian culture. The villagers understood that their beloved swami was passing through a dangerous stage of his sadhana, one that required their understanding and support. Eventually they learned a trick that reliably got Swami Kripalu back on track.

Approaching him they would say, "Swami, it is time for your sadhana." Hearing this, Swami Kripalu would cease whatever he was doing and allow himself to be escorted back to his meditation room, where he would resume his practice.

One day, while lost to the external world in a transcendental state, Swami Kripalu wandered away. Not wearing any clothes, he passed through several neighboring villages. When some of Swami Kripalu's devotees heard that a naked saint was roaming the area, they suspected it might be their guru. Finding and escorting him back home, they were afraid he might wander off again. Several devotees agreed to keep a constant vigil for the rest of the night, sitting with Swami Kripalu on the banks of the Narmada river. A few hours had passed when Swami Kripalu, who had been sitting quietly in meditation, all of a sudden and without any warning stood up and dove into the river.

The Narmada is one of India's largest rivers, and it was well into monsoon season. The waters were surging with strong currents, and Swami Kripalu was instantly carried away. Disappearing into the dark of a moonless night, the villagers who witnessed that event felt certain his life was lost and a few started to cry.

"We are not helping him by crying," yelled one villager. "Let's form a search party and proceed along the river bank toward Shinor. With dawn approaching, there is still some hope we may find him." They began running along the bank, lanterns darting through the night like fireflies.

Meanwhile, Swami Kripalu was being swept downstream at a rapid pace, tossed about by a raging current, and frequently pulled under water. For quite some time, he struggled with all his might, trying to stay afloat and keep from drowning. Since he had eaten and slept little for days, exhaustion was overtaking him. His hands and feet grew numb. Facing death, Swami Kripalu cried out over the roar of the water, "Gurudev, I am drowning. Please save me!"

As if Swami Kripalu's plea was instantly received, he heard a voice respond out of the dark night, a voice that he somehow could hear over the roar of the raging river. "Swami, stop swimming." Certain his mind was failing, and that this was a hallucination, he kept on struggling. But again, he heard the voice, "Swami, stop swimming; surrender."

Swami Kripalu recognized his guru's familiar voice and experienced a moment of relief. Gathering his courage, he gave up his struggle, relinquishing any effort to swim or stay above the surface. As soon as he stopped moving his arms and legs, his body became buoyant and floated easily atop the raging torrent. All fear of drowning disappeared and a feeling of triumph and ecstasy swept through him. Spontaneously, he started chanting:

Om Namah Shivay Gurave
 (I bow to thee, Lord Shiva, in the form of the guru)
Sacchidananda Murtaye
(Embodiment of existence, consciousness, and bliss)
Namastasmai Namastasmai Namastasmai
(I bow to thee. I bow to thee. I bow to thee)
Namo Namah
(Respectfully I bow)

His body was now gently drifting upon the water's surface like a flower. The river broadened and he was able to glide from one bank to the other. Relaxed and enjoying a peace unknown to him, he floated this way for an hour or more. It was morning when he approached the shore near Shinor. The search party was anxiously waiting there, unable to believe their eyes as he floated into shore, alive and unscathed. The eyes of the villagers brimmed with tears of joy, and he met their glances with an untroubled smile.

Swami Kripalu returned to the village where he resumed his sadhana, once again interspersed with time for rest and refreshment. Having tasted true surrender, he was able to explore the higher stages of yoga. No longer a source of concern or disturbance, Swami Kripalu's presence was a boon to the village in every way, and it quickly became recognized as the home of a great saint and yogi.

Commentary

Like many spiritual adepts, Swami Kripalu's life involved a great vow to achieve enlightenment, followed by a great struggle, and ultimately a great realization. His journey down the river was a defining moment, enabling him to navigate the difficult transition from willful practice to surrender.

It is important to note that Swami Kripalu was treading the path of Pashupat kundalini yoga in which willful practices are done until the life force of the body has been sufficiently activated. That accomplished, practice shifts entirely to surrender. In Kripalu Yoga, no such clear line of demarcation exists. From the outset of practice, there is a continual blending of will and surrender. Yet this story remains pertinent, as Kripalu Yoga practitioners must still learn to navigate across the threshold of mind-based, volitional activity into states of flow of surrender.

Swami Kripalu never described himself as a liberated soul, yet he radiated a palpable energy of compassionate love and spiritual power that profoundly impacted those who came into his presence. Another of his bhajans provides a window onto the nature of Swami Kripalu's transformation.

Since experiencing the vision of the Sustainer of the Universe, I have awakened from my deep slumber and see his beautiful form everywhere in flashes of awakening.

Preparing a garland, I eagerly wait to offer it to the Lord.
Suddenly, I see him smiling in the garland.
Finding his form everywhere I turn, to whom can I offer my garland?

43

When I light the ghee lamp for the Lord
My eyes suddenly meet his in the flame.
When the whole universe is filled with the Lord,
To whom can I offer my arti?

Looking at my face in the mirror,
I find that I have become one with the life of the universe.
That Merciful One has made me one with himself.
To whom can I offer my devotion?

History

The events narrated in this story occurred in the village of Rajpipla during the late 1950s when Swami Kripalu was in his mid-forties. When telling this story, it was obvious that Swami Kripalu's amazement at surviving this ordeal never left him.

For a quality soundtrack of the Shiva Mantra spontaneously chanted by Swami Kripalu while floating down the Narmada, see *Soul Flight: Chanted Mantras for Healing and Illumination* by Bhavani Lorraine Nelson.

For a contemporary biography written by a senior member of the Kripalu Yoga community, see *Pilgrim of Love: The Life and Teachings of Swami Kripalu by* Atma Jo Ann Levitt (Monkfish Book Publishing Company 2004). See also *Sayings of Swami Kripalu: Inspiring Quotes from a Contemporary Yoga Master,* edited by Richard Faulds (Peaceable Kingdom Books 2004).

Chapter Four

Names are Many, Truth is One

Swami Kripalu's guru was a magical figure. Legend has it that two months prior to meeting Swami Kripalu, he wandered into Bombay carrying only a water pot. After miraculously saving the life of a wealthy businessman's son, he was provided a stately mansion to use as an ashram. Recognized as a great soul, he was quickly surrounded by a retinue of devotees. No one knew his name, so they called him "Gurudev."

When asked by Swami Kripalu to reveal his name, the guru advised the youth to chant the pranav mantra, better known as the sacred syllable Om. The implication was that through mantra meditation Swami Kripalu could learn firsthand who he was. After this response, Swami Kripalu chose to call him *Pranavanda*.

At the end of his 15 month tutelage, Pranavanada took Swami Kripalu on a pilgrimage. In accord with tradition, the two traveled by foot, eating once a day, and speaking only in the evening on religious topics, visiting the many holy places associated with Lord Krishna, an incarnation of Vishnu.

The pilgrimage took several days, their route tracing the life of Krishna. They embarked at Krishna's birthplace, continued to where he spent his childhood, and ended in the city where Krishna served as a high-ranking minister in the ruling court. Each day the two walked many miles, visiting places where Krishna had performed amazing feats.

This story reflects just one of many amazing experience Swami Kripalu had while traveling with his guru.

A Lesson in Monotheism

After a long day's walk, the two pilgrims wended their way into Vrindavan. It was time for the evening ceremony of offering the light called *arti*. Assuming the nearby temple was dedicated to Krishna, Swami Kripalu entered and was surprised to find it adorned with a Shiva lingam.

After finishing prayers, Swami Kripalu came out and sat down next to his guru in the temple courtyard. Night had fallen and conversation was now permitted. Swami Kripalu asked, "Since Vrindavan is Lord Krishna's abode, why is there a temple for Lord Shiva here?"

Pranavanda responded, "Are you talking in your sleep?"

Swami Kripalu pressed, "I asked and will ask again, why this temple dedicated to Lord Shiva?"

Pranavanda's reply sounded exasperated, "You seem to be fallen under some delusion about the deity."

Swami Kripalu was confounded, "No sir, I had a proper look at the lingam and even questioned a devotee also attending prayers. It is a Shiva temple."

Pranavanda proffered an obvious way to resolve the dispute, "All right, go inside and have another look so that you might come out of your delusion."

Swami Kripalu went inside the temple and beheld an idol of Lord Krishna. Rubbing his eyes to make sure he was not imagining things, he went back out to his guru. Pranavanda asked with a smile, "Well, what did you see?"

With some embarrassment, Swami Kripalu said, "There's an idol of Lord Krishna in there."

Now laughing, Pranavanda said, "Swami, you are not making any sense. Please go in again and remove your delusion."

As directed, Swami Kripalu went inside yet again. This time he found both an idol of Krishna and a lingam, installed side by side. He came out quite dazed, and sat down before Pranavanda, clasping his head in both hands, totally beside himself and speechless.

Pranavanda asked him: "Did you see it properly this time? What is it, an idol or a lingam?"

Swami Kripalu could only stammer out one word, "Both."

Pranavanda's eyes twinkled, " Has something gone wrong with your eyes? You say something different each time."

Swami Kripalu became annoyed and retorted, "My eyes are perfectly fine, but you seem to have cast a spell on them because I keep seeing different things at different times."

Hearing Swami Kripalu's annoyance, Pranavanda affectionately stroked his head and said, "All right, go inside a final time. Whichever form of God you see, take him to be the presiding deity of this temple."

Reluctantly, Swami Kripalu went inside a fourth time. There was only the lingam that he had seen initially. The temple priest was there, who he asked to make sure. Returning to Pranavanda, Swami Kripalu said, "I was right the first time. A lingam is installed in this Shiva temple."

Pranavanda countered his smugness, "Then how is it that you saw the idol of Lord Krishna? And once you even said that both an idol and a lingam were inside the temple. Please explain how could that happen?"

Swami Kripalu answered, "I've no explanation. Please do me the favor of explaining this phenomenon."

Pranavanda replied, "Swami, when you first went inside the temple, you saw Lord Shiva there. The next time you saw Lord Krishna. And the third time you saw both of them side by side. What does this indicate? It shows that one form of God is not different from another. Nor is any form of God superior to others. All forms of God are of equal importance."

"I am enunciating the principle of monotheism for you today, so you do not get entangled in the web of sectarianism. Victims of narrow sectarianism can never acquire true comprehension or real devotion."

"Since you have been born and brought up as a Vaishnav, I've asked you to keep the form of Krishna as the main deity on your altar. However, you should also consider Shiva as the deity and worship the lingam. It can be said that Hara, Lord Shiva, and Hari, Lord Vishnu, are one and the same. I made you witness this miracle so you could acquire an unshakable faith in the principle of monotheism."

Swami Kripalu asked, "After leaving Bombay, why did you select this area for our pilgrimage?"

Pranvanada replied, "Because of you."

"Why because of me?" Swami Kripalu said with surprise.

"Because I want to strengthen the inherited and existing traits in you," answered Pranavanada.

Swami Kripalu continued his inquiry, "What if I had inherited Shaivite traits instead of Vaishnav traits?"

"In that case I would have taken you on a pilgrimage to Kashi, Haridwar, and Rishikesh, the places holy to Lord Shiva," answered Pranavanda.

Taking this in, Swami Kripalu protested, "But doesn't this amount to strengthening sectarianism? To strengthen the spirit of monotheism, shouldn't a person with my traits be taken to the land of Shiva?"

"While noble, your idea is not correct. To practice sadhana, it is essential for a yogi to have unflinching faith in his chosen form of God. Faith in the form to which one has established an emotional bond since childhood can easily be made stronger. Although effort can rouse faith in a different form, it is less likely to prove strong enough to survive the rigors of sadhana. So the best approach is to build upon existing traits."

"Moreover, as true faith arises with spiritual experience, an objective viewpoint is developed, and other forms of God will not be considered inferior. Thus this approach is the best basis to cultivate a mature monotheism. Remember, a faith aroused by narrow sectarianism is not true faith. It is a blind faith subject to fanaticism, and not conducive to love. One who truly loves God considers all religions, sects, and human beings as equal. This is true monotheism."

As Swami Kripalu's doubts cleared, his drowsiness increased and soon he was fast asleep.

Commentary

Hinduism is known for its religious tolerance, which is often thought to result from a pantheistic view of a universe populated by many gods and goddesses. As illustrated by this story, the tolerance of a mature Hindu is grounded in an understanding of monotheism, which believes in an underlying oneness that precludes sectarianism.

While founded upon monotheism, yoga practice in the Kripalu tradition is intended to lead one to *monism*. Yogic monism arises from the inner experience that all things arise from a single cause or essence. Although reflective of this experiential truth, monotheism is an abstract principle meant to inform spiritual practice. Monism is direct knowing, existing beyond the realm of conceptual thought.

Swami Kripalu was a *bhakti yogi*, someone of a devotional nature who relates to the infinite as a Supreme Being. The Kripalu tradition recognizes that there are individuals who are intellectually-oriented (*jnani yogis*) and others who are action-oriented (*karma yogis*). A yogi's beliefs and practices must reflect his or her nature, and individuals of these types are likely to be of a more scientific or pragmatic bent. Their orientation toward deeper reality might take the form of a search for truth, or an exploration of the motivating power behind all actions. Interestingly, traditional theism is not required for yogic monotheism.

It was by watering the seed of devotion that Swami Kripalu's bhakti practice sprouted and grew to include the other major elements of yoga. A close Western disciple, Yogeshwar Muni, formely Charles Berner, taught a three-step technique of devotional meditation informed by the teachings of Swami Kripalu that leads from monotheism to monism.

First the meditator "gets a sense of himself or herself." This means consciously registering the felt sense of your body, the quality of heart and mind, and anything else that is true for you in the moment. There is no attempt to change anything, just the process of establishing contact with "the actuality." In Kripalu Yoga terms, this is equivalent to bringing yourself present.

The second step is to open to the Divine. The Divine can be conceptualized as infinite love, energy, truth, consciousness, radiant emptiness, or anything else that calls to you. This is a process of opening to the ideal and sacred, an aspect of existence that is perfect, whole and complete.

In consciously connecting the finite and the infinite, you will experience that there is a flow of energy that emanates from the Divine to inform the bodymind. Staying attuned to this source energy, surrender to it completely and simply witness whatever results. Allowing this energetic flow to steadily evolve your being is the practice, and anything needing to happen will occur naturally. Staying with the practice, a state of communion arises that ultimately leads beyond itself to union.

The direct experience of union, sometimes called Absolute Unitary Being, is universal. Such direct experience takes one beyond concepts, even those like monotheism that comprise the spiritual path walked to arrive there.

Although raised in rural India, Swami Kripalu was well read, praised people of discrimination and discernment, and considered himself "scientifically minded." It appears he had some difficulty reconciling this with the many miracles he experienced, especially with his teacher in his younger years. He only told these miracle stories to a small number of close disciples, and forbade them from repeating them publicly.

Only late in his life, in response to the pleas of many devotees, did Swami Kripalu grant permission for these stories to be published after his death.

History

Scholars know the Pashupats were monotheists, envisioning the Lord as the creator, sustainer, and destroyer of the universe. In orthodox Hinduism, these three aspects of the divine are viewed as a trinity of Gods, those being Brahma the creator, Vishnu the sustainer, and Shiva the destroyer. Many add the Goddess as a fourth and equal expression.

These are all examples of what is called *Saguna Brahman,* the ultimate reality expressed with attributes in form. Hinduism also recognizes *Nirguna Brahman,* the ultimate reality in its pure and transcendental state, which is formless and devoid of any attributes or qualities. Although a minority of individuals easily relate to the idea of a formless God, the traditional path was to choose a form of God to worship and ultimately go beyond it.

Beginning with monotheism, Swami Kripalu conveyed the essence of Pranavananda's instruction in *Premyatra, Pilgrimage of Love* as follows: "Now I would like to describe to you in short the guidance that my beloved Guru gave to me: Believe in the presence of God and accept his non-dual nature. To the best of your ability, obey yama and niyama. Pray, recite mantra, perform worship, and sing devotional songs. Eat and speak moderately. Practice postures, pranayama, and meditation according to your capacity. Study, ponder and digest the scriptures. Keep the company of saints. Practice self-discipline, self-observation and virtuous conduct."

Chapter Five

No Solid Self

While living in the ashram, Swami Kripalu grew curious about his guru's past. Pranavananda would only say, "It is not proper to ask an ascetic about his prior life. Having renounced everything, he does not have any relationship with his past." The unwavering tone of Pranavanda's voice led Swami Kripalu to set aside his desire, accepting the fact that his curiosity would not be satisfied directly.

Some months later, a gentleman came to the ashram seeking to meet the saint whose fame was quickly spreading in Bombay's spiritual circles. When entering the room for audience, Pranavananda recognized the visitor as a longtime friend. Through the visitor, Swami Kripalu learned much about his guru, including this story of his initiation onto the path of yoga.

Bathing the Guru

Pranavananda's former name was Bankimbabu. He and his wife of 17 years, Ashadevi, lived in Calcutta. Well placed in society, the couple had only one regret: they were childless.

A friend suggested they make one of the most difficult of all Hindu pilgrimage, traveling by foot to a remote Shiva temple in the Himalayas. Deeply involved in his work and skeptical of such notions, Bankimbabu was not interested. Years passed and Ashadevi grew depressed because any likelihood of her motherhood was disappearing. Giving in to his wife's repeated request, the two made the difficult journey to the temple and offered their sincere prayers.

On their return, calamity struck in a desolate spot. Bankimbabu suddenly collapsed and lost all consciousness. Ashadevi, holding her husband's head in her lap, watched the life ebb out of his body. Crying out for help, she was amazed to see a radiant monk step from the brush into the clearing.

Sprinkling Bankimbabu's face with water, then staring steadily into his closed eyes for a few minutes, the monk was able to revive him. Within a short time, Bankimbabu was back on his feet. Ashadevi narrated the events of his recovery and Bankimbabu fell prostrate at the feet of the holy man, saying, "We are greatly indebted to you, but how can we repay you in this barren place? Kindly come with us to Calcutta and give us an opportunity to serve you there."

The monk responded, "I shall keep that in mind and come to Calcutta someday." Turning and walking back into the brush, he was gone as suddenly as he appeared. Realizing that they had not offered him any gift or told him their address, Bankimbabu and Ashadevi were dismayed but there was nothing left to do but proceed on their way.

Three months later, Bankimbabu was greeted by the monk, who was standing outside the entrance way of his house. He immediately called Ashadevi, who escorted the monk to the sitting room, where Bankimbabu and Ashadevi sat at his feet.

Bankimbabu said, "We are extremely blessed to have you visit our home and you are welcome to stay with us as long as you like. Too indebted to ever repay you, we surrender at your holy feet." Ashadevi brought fruits, sweets, and milk to their guest.

"I shall only stay with you for a day, and this body does not require food," the monk responded.

Ashadevi was distressed to not be able to provide hospitality to her guest and said, "How can one live without food or water? You must take food sometimes? If it does not suit you now, please take it whenever you like."

The monk responded by taking a single basil leaf, which he put into his mouth. "I have accepted your hospitality through this leaf. Don't worry about my food, and you should also observe a fast today.

"We are not worried about our food, but want to spend time conversing with you," said Bankimbabu. "By what name shall we call you?"

"You may call me by any name. Address me as convenient, and I will not object to any name you chose to call me."

"Then I shall call you Bhagwan (Lord)," said Bankimbabu.

As the conversation continued, Bankimbabu indirectly mentioned the couple's secret desire. "Bhagwan, we undertook the pilgrimage to fulfill one desire. Although it may or may not be fulfilled, it has certainly benefited us by providing an opportunity to meet you, especially now that you have favored us with a visit to our home. We are infinitely blessed."

The monk simply raised his hand, saying, "Son, one year from now you will have a child."

Both husband and wife were overjoyed, and Bankimbabu gratefully said, "Thank you, and kindly bless us with guidance for our spiritual progress, according to our capacity."

"It is enough for householders pursuing a path of success in life to regularly recite the name of God, and I will give you mantra initiation in the evening. Another initiation is required to tread the path of liberation."

Bankimbabu said, "I would very much like to try for liberation but am not aware of my competence. If you find me qualified, I will pursue the path of liberation."

"The path of liberation requires special effort and the abandoning of worldly duties," said the monk, looking pointedly at Ashadevi.

"No woman wants her husband to become an ascetic. Yet I am not so selfish as to hinder the welfare of his soul," said Ashadevi.

"Your thoughts are noble, and I am pleased with you," said the monk. "Bankimbabu shall do mantra recitation while leading his householder life. This will weaken his attachments and prepare him for the path of liberation. In due time, I will give him the appropriate initiation."

Such had passed the conversation when the monk said, "It's time for me to sit in meditation. You carry on with your routines. Half an hour before the sun sets, I'll get up and have a bath. Then I'll give you mantra initiation, which is why I asked you to fast today."

Ashadevi arranged a carpet in the guest room for the monk to sit. The couple went about their daily chores, eagerly awaiting the appointed hour. As evening approached, they bathed and waited for the monk to rise from meditation. He came out with his water pot in hand, and Bankimbabu led him to the bathroom, where Ashadevi had prepared two large buckets of hot water for his bath.

The monk asked them to bring a large tub and place it in the center of the room. With this done, the monk instructed them, "I'll sit in the tub and you two will bathe me. Ashadevi will pour water on my body, and Bankimbabu will rub it clean. Do not be frightened or stop if anything strange happens during the bath. Use all the water from both buckets. When you are finished, pour the collected water into my water pot. Fill it up to the brim and bring it to my room." The monk then sat in the tub, crossing his legs in lotus posture. As the couple began the bath, he closed his eyes in meditation.

Ashadevi poured the water, and Bankimbabu started rubbing his body. They were startled to discover that his skin began peeling off, revealing white underneath like a boiled potato. Though frightened and astounded, they continued as instructed. With all the skin removed, the monk's body resembled a marble statue, but it was soft like a banana. As they continued, the white of the body started melting in the poured water, leaving a round white ball, which finally dissolved completely into the water.

Except for the monk's prayer beads and loin cloth, the tub was now full of water that appeared like milk. Continuing as directed, they began pouring the water from the tub into the water pot. Much to their surprise, they were able to pour all the water from the large tub into the small water pot. Taking the water pot, beads and loin cloth to the guest room, Bankimbabu and Ashadevi were astonished to find the monk sitting there, eyes closed in meditation. They went close and bowed in reverence.

The monk opened his eyes and with a smile said, "My children, you inquired about the needs of my body this morning, so I made you witness this strange bath in order to give you some idea about it. I hope now you have rightly perceived its

57

nature." He lovingly placed his hand upon their heads and said, "Now I will give you mantra initiation."

Regaining their composure, they sat before the monk, who then conferred the twelve-syllable Krishna mantra, Om Namo Bhagavate Vasudevaya. (I bow to the Lord in the form of Vasudeva's Son)

Bankimbabu became inquisitive and asked, "Bhagwan, you have promised to guide me in the pursuit of liberation today. When will I be so favored, and what is the nature of this pursuit?"

"Liberation is accomplished through yoga, and it is not proper to give yoga initiation to one who has not qualified for it. Mantra recitation will purify your body and mind, and you will be qualified when they are sufficiently purified, explained the monk.

Reflecting on their initiation, Ashadevi said, "We have been calling you Bhagwan, and now you are our guru too. So hereafter we shall call you Guru Bhagwan.

Guru Bhagwan had already departed when Bankimbabu and Ashadevi awoke early the next morning. One year later, Ashadevi gave birth to a daughter they named Kamlesh. Not long thereafter, Bankimbabu left home with his wife's blessing to pursue the path of yoga.

Commentary

This strange tale uses a simple yet effective ploy to conceal its deeper meaning. While the story line is about mantra initiation for householders, its content describes the initiation into yoga pointedly declared to be secret. The result is that listeners taking the story at face value are distracted from probing more deeply, while those awake to symbolism can decipher a message needed to go further in their practice.

The story opens with a classic theme: when the student is ready, the guru appears. In this instance, the guru not only appears in the nick of time to save Bankimbabu's life, he goes out of his way to visit their Calcutta home. This expresses the traditional view that a person focused on fulfilling his or her duties in life will be called to the spiritual path when the time is right.

The story continues by affirming traditional distinctions between men, women, householders and renunciate monks. Motherhood, along with mantra initiation, represents the fulfillment of Ashadevi's life as a woman. Guru Bhagwan grants the couple a boon by blessing their efforts to conceive a child. Bankimbabu aspires to walk the path of liberation, which will ultimately require him to abandon his family.

Readers may find it surprising that married spiritual seekers were not encouraged to practice yoga. They were advised to live an energetic, virtuous, and successful family life. Householders wanting to grow spiritually were given mantra initiation and told to practice mantra recitation each morning and evening. Swami Kripalu expanded this traditional view, permitting earnest householders to practice yoga, pranayama, and meditation for up to one hour, mornings and evenings. He cautioned anyone engaging in this amount of practice to understand that they would gradually grow disinterested with worldly life. Kripalu Yoga was developed in America as a potent spiritual practice for people living active lives. Thus it represents a further extension of the tradition.

The story continues to paint a fascinating picture of depth spiritual practice. Yoga is an initiatory tradition, and the story makes clear that teachings are transmitted from guru to disciple only after a proper ceremony is performed. In India, initiation is not considered a formality. Along with a spiritual blessing, it established a context for instruction in a transformative practice, ongoing guidance and correction, and the validation of results. The term for this type of initiatory practice in the Kripalu tradition is *sadhana,* which means *the systematic practice of yogic disciplines for self-transformation.*

In the bathing scene, the three participants enact what occurs in sadhana. With transformation traditionally seen as a process of purification, bathing is a fit metaphor. Sitting in the bathtub, the guru is the person doing the practice. He crosses his legs, closes his eyes, and sits in meditation. Ashadevi and Bankimbabu represent the process itself, one of removing layers upon layers that obscure the Self.

Midway through the bath, the guru's skin and flesh have dissolved, leaving a round white ball. This represents the deeper sense of self that lies beneath the thinking mind and ego. A practitioner might think this is the true self. But as the bath continues, this also dissolves and Ashadevi and Bankimbabu are astounded to find that there is no personal self. All that remains is a milk-like liquid, a symbol of vast, undifferentiated, and primordial awareness.

The story's conclusion beautifully expresses the paradoxical nature of depth spiritual experience. After realizing that one is nothing other than the radiant emptiness of Self, daily life goes on. Somehow all that awareness fits into the water pot of the bodymind. Carrying the pot into the next room, the guru is there as before, embodied and interacting through the vehicle of a personality and character. Yet the guru is different from the student; he knows who he is, and that knowing informs how he conducts himself in life

It is noteworthy that the guru is able to provide accurate and detailed instructions to Ashadevi and Bankimbabu. The value of such competence, which can only be acquired by personally going through the transformative process, cannot be underestimated. Guru Bhagwan's advice is worth remembering by any spiritual practitioner: "Do not be frightened or stop if anything strange happens... Use all the water from both buckets." A spiritual practice must engaged in without interruption and carried through to completion to effect its intended transformation. This always entails passing beyond comfort zones to confront the unknown and unexpected.

History

A literal interpretation of this story is that it reveals the nature of a *nirmandeha*. This is a body created out of thought by a guru, which can be used to travel instantly to distant locations, and appear in several places at once. At other times, a yoga adept is said to be able to enter and revitalize a recently dead body, using it as a temporary instrument to accomplish desired objectives. In this view, all the miracle working gurus of the Kripalu tradition are seen as aspects of Lakulish.

Although given a spiritual name for convenience sake, the intention of a renunciate monk is to realize his or her deeper identity beyond name or form. Thus a realized guru may shun the use of any particular name and identify completely with the deity.

Chapter Six

Swimming with Krishna

The life and exploits of the god-man Krishna are depicted in two Indian epics, the *Mahabharata* and *Srimad Bhagavatam*. Each is a treasure trove of Indian mythology and spirituality.

An avatar of Lord Vishnu, Krishna grew up as a cowherd in the rural village of Vrindhivan. Sudama and Krishna were childhood friends who spent their days playing in the fields while watching over the village's calves. Upon coming of age, Krishna moved to the ruling city of Hastina and later Dwarka, where he took up his task of ridding the world of evildoers. While Sudama remained behind, the affection between the two never lapsed.

Krishna Visits Sudama

One day Krishna, weary of his complicated life in the city, thought to himself, "I have not seen my friend Sudama for a very long time. If I call him here, he will not feel at ease because I am a king and he is a pauper. So I shall go to his home." Calling his attendants, Krishna declared, "I am going on a secret journey and will return in a few days."

Sudama's home was small and his existence simple. There was not a single sweet snack anywhere to even look at, and it was not unusual for two or three days to pass during which he offered prayers while living on only yawns. Sudama was content to live in this manner because it helped him pray with a humble heart.

It is said that Laxmi, the Goddess of Wealth, once appeared to Sudama in all her finery. She wanted to show her pleasure

62

with Sudama's unwavering devotion by granting him a boon. Sudama greeted her warmly, saying, "Mother, if you wish to visit this house, you are always welcome, but please come in simple dress and be willing to live like me. You go pray in that corner of the house, and I will pray in this corner. I don't want wealth or luxury. All I want to be is a devotee. "

As twilight waned over the house of Sudama, Krishna knocked at the door, garbed in the dress of a cowherd to conceal his identity. Sudama was engrossed in meditation, and his wife, Maina, was bustling about doing housework. On hearing the knock, Maina opened the door and Krishna affectionately disclosed the purpose of his visit. "Sister," said Krishna. "I have sneaked away just to be with you and Sudama. Can I please stay here for a few days?"

Maina was overwhelmed with joy. She welcomed Krishna lovingly, giving him a basin of water in which to wash his face and hands. After bathing, he sat down on a ragged mat in the courtyard and tasted the water from the jug Maina had placed beside him. Krishna said, "Sister, to tell you the truth, your water is sweeter than that of Dwarka."

With a knowing smile, Maina replied, "Your statement is true only because Dwarka's water is not water. The water is turned into nectar wherever you reside. After drinking nectar all the time, it is only natural for the water of a friend's house to taste better as a welcome change of pace."

"Sister," laughed Krishna, "let us drop this subject and get to the point. What you are going to serve me to eat tonight?" Sudama's wife replied with a smile, "Rice and beans with spinach curry," to which Krishna exclaimed, "My favorite food!"

As Sudama exited the meditation room, his delight knew no bounds at the sight of Krishna sitting in his courtyard. Embracing warmly, the two friends allowed tears of love to flow unabashedly from their eyes. Over and over, Sudama murmured, "Krishna! Krishna! Krishna!" And Krishna answered, "Sudama! Sudama! Sudama!" More than words, these were streams of love flowing between two united hearts.

The two began to talk and talk. They continued talking through dinner, eating a little, then talking a lot, then eating a little, and talking a lot more. For quite a few hours, they were completely oblivious of the passage of time. Even after going to bed, they kept talking and talking. Midnight came, and Maina reminded her husband, "Our brother has traveled a long way by a secret route. He must be tired, so let him rest for a while."

But Krishna objected. "Sister, you go to sleep peacefully. Although I am now a king, you seem to have forgotten that I was once a shepherd. Taking care of the cows required my running to and fro all day long. It was common for me to climb up and down Mount Govardhana several times a day. I have not grown so enfeebled to be fatigued by an ordinary trip. Anyway, I have been dreaming every night of my good friend, Sudama, while in Dwarka. Now that I am here face to face with him, sleep will not come. So why don't you let us talk?" Thus, their speech flowed continuously and no one slept.

The next day, Krishna was delighted to play for hours with Sudama's children. Joyous sounds echoed throughout the house as Krishna bounced them in his lap and made them smile and laugh in innumerable ways.

On the third day, Krishna and Sudama set out to have a bath in the lake. As they walked, Sudama reflected, "Krishna is yogi who has realized the highest truth. Many consider him an incarnation of Lord Vishnu himself. Now that he is right here with me, why shouldn't I ask Krishna to enlighten me to the divine illusion (maya) underlying this world? So Sudama said, "Krishna, I have been told that you have revealed your maya to many sages and saints. Please show it to me."

Krishna smiled and advised, "Set such talk aside and know that my maya is not worth seeing." Sudama was not satisfied with this answer, and continued to press, "Please don't avoid my request. I am your best friend, so it is not proper that I should go without seeing it."

Before they had left for their bath, Sudama's wife had told them, "Remember that the meal is almost ready, so don't take long. The only thing left for me to do is to roll the chappatis. I will not do this until you come back, so they will be hot for you."

Krishna replied, "If you keep on talking about this subject, it is likely that we will be late for dinner." But Sudama persisted in his demand, "Forget the chappatis, and tell me right now whether you intend to show me your maya or not."

"I am not at all opposed to revealing my maya to you," replied Krishna. "I only hesitate because I fear that you will regret the experience." Sudama said, "I want to find out for myself." To which Krishna responded, "Then I will reveal it." Sudama smiled in anticipation.

By now they had reached the lake. As they walked into the water, Krishna asked, "Sudama, how long can you hold your breath under water? Let's have a contest!"

"But brother," stammered Sudama. "You are an accomplished

warrior and a yogi. I am a peasant and devotee. You can undoubtedly hold your breath longer than me." "No doubt about it," said Krishna. "Then let's experiment," said Sudama. "We will dive together."

Now standing in deep water, they faced each other, took a deep breath, and dropped beneath the surface. At that moment, Krishna fulfilled his promise and revealed the great illusion to Sudama.

Sudama held his breath for some time, but was soon forced to come up for air. Although he saw many people bathing on the shore, he could not find Krishna. After waiting for several minutes, he wondered, "Where has Krishna gone? We both dove underwater at the same moment." An hour passed, but Krishna was nowhere in sight.

Sudama walked out of the water, and noticed with some surprise that he was standing on an unfamiliar beach on the outskirts of an unknown city. He thought, "Maybe I am confused and remembering a time in the past when I was with Krishna." So he walked into the city and gave the name of his hometown to two or three people, asking, "How far is it from here?"

Each replied, "Brother, I have never in my life heard of any such place and regret that I am unable to tell you how far it is from here." After some time, Sudama had no choice but to settle down in that city. Eventually he forgot all about his wife and children. Since one must work at some job to make a living, he engaged himself in an occupation and eventually achieved success. Some time later, he married and began raising a family.

In that city, people observed a special custom upon the death of a married woman. Her husband was cremated along with her body. One day Sudama's wife suddenly died. Several neighbors grabbed his arms to escort him to the funeral pyre so he would not run away.

Sudama had no intention of being cremated in this way. Feigning cooperation, he devised an escape plan and asked his captors, "The river is nearby. Would you let me bathe and purify my soul of sins before we proceed with my funeral?" His plan was to dive into the water and swim away.

His captors consented. Sudama, dwelling on the name of the Lord, dove into the river and swam underwater as far as he could go. When he could no longer hold his breath, his head popped out of the water, his face etched with terror, certain he would be pursued and killed by his captors.

Then, all of a sudden, right beside him, was Krishna. He threw his arms around Krishna, who let a few moments pass before asking, "Sudama, why do you look so scared?" "Why shouldn't I be terrified, shouted Sudama, they are going to cremate me with my dead wife!"

"Sudama! What kind of crazy talk is that? Sister is in the kitchen. Where is this funeral you are talking about, and who are these people who are going to cremate you?"

Jolted into silence, Sudama stared awestruck at Krishna's face and began to mutter to himself. "Then what on earth did I see?" Sudama folded his hands in prayer and pleaded, "Oh Krishna! Please don't show me your maya ever again."

Krishna chuckled. "No, no. Come now, you must see it again, just one more time." Sudama wailed, "No, Brother, no. For my sake, please don't ever show me your maya again."

'Then let's go home," said Krishna, "Maina will be waiting and we will be right on time for dinner. Your dive lasted only six minutes."

Sudama was incredulous, "I lived a whole fifty years in just six minutes. Krishna, your maya is extraordinary."

Commentary

Like many religious myths, this story has two levels of meaning. The first offers a reassuring perspective on life to a person of simple faith. While it may appear that God is distant, he is actually right beside us as we earn a living, raise our family, and eventually prepare to face death. Conceptions or God as a personal savior of the devout, or a miracle working yogi able to intervene when loyal devotees are facing difficulties, further add to this view.

The second meaning is meant for those of a mystical bent, offering clues on how to awaken to a deeper experience of reality. This story graphically describes the nature of maya, or illusion. Elsewhere in the *Srimad Bhagatam*, Krishna states the same message more directly: "The eternal soul is pure and permanent, something apart from the constantly changing things of this world. Because of maya, individuals are deluded into thinking they are involved in the play of the three *gunas*. If a man wants to attain liberation, he should try to realize this world to be an illusion, like a waking man realizes the dream world is an illusion. To do this, he should learn to control the senses, steady the mind, and practice the eight limbs of yoga."

Indian metaphysics posits that there are three gunas or elemental forces underlying the physical universe. Because they exist in an unstable balance, the world is always shifting and changing. Maya derives its power over us when we believing ourselves to be the body and mind, which casts us as a character in the great drama of life. To wake up, we must identify with the soul, which exists beyond the three gunas *(triguna titha)* and is always in union with God.

A devotee of Lord Krishna, Swami Kripalu described his own journey in these terms, saying "Maya is quite extraordinary. Indeed, the Lord's play is totally beyond our grasp. The merciful Lord graciously revealed his maya to me. Still to this day, I cannot imagine why."

History

It appears that Krishna and Sudama lived circa 2000 B.C.E. Narrating the events of an earlier age, the *Mahabharat* and *Srimad Bhagavatam* were composed over many generations and did not appear in final form until the second or third century C.E.

Chapter Seven

Mastery in Teaching

Swami Kripalu held teachers in high esteem, praising their work as essential to society. He believed that anyone with a love for learning who teaches from a place of genuine caring for students is answering a lofty call, whether serving as a kindergarten instructor, a university professor, a career mentor, or a spiritual guide.

While honoring all teachers, Swami Kripalu distinguished between teachers and *acharyas*. Acharyas are extraordinary teachers whose depth of study and practice has purified their character. The presence of such a person becomes edifying, making their life and example their foremost teaching.

Although any teacher can become an acharya, it requires the willingness to remain a perpetual student. Acharyas must also master the art of imparting knowledge by heightening their sensitivity to the individual needs and learning styles of students.

This is the story of one such master teacher, an acharya whose task was to ensure that the rulers of a kingdom remained noble and virtuous.

Whipping the Prince

Once there was a wise Acharya who had served the royal family for many years. His character was noble, and in difficult situations his counsel almost always proved correct. Accordingly, the King hardly ever acted contrary to his advice.

After teaching the Prince for many years, the Acharya was told by the King that it was time for his son to assume the throne. A happy Acharya determined an auspicious day for the coronation ceremony.

When the appointed day arrived, the entire kingdom was making merry, honoring the long rule of a righteous King and celebrating the crowning of a humble and deserving Prince.

The servants carefully bathed the Prince and were in the early stages of dressing him in his finery when a message came from the Acharya: "Come immediately to your study room."

The Prince thought, "Why does my Acharya call me? Surely it is not to engage in routine study on this day. Perhaps he is going to give me a special teaching." Moments after sending a reply that he was coming, the Prince started walking, clad only in his lower cloth. Arriving, he bowed low before his Acharya. As he bent forward, the Acharya delivered five strong blows with a long leather lash on his bare back.

The prince did not understand why he was punished so severely. He thought to himself, "Normally when my guru tells me something, he makes his point gently. Today, he delivered the most severe physical punishment without saying anything. Although he didn't appear angry, I must have made some mistake somewhere."

As he stood back up, he looked closely at the face of his longtime teacher. The Acharya appeared completely balanced and peaceful, with no disturbance on his face or turmoil in his being. In fact, the Acharya was looking very kindly back into his eyes. The Prince had great respect for his Acharya and knew that he was not an impulsive or cruel person.

From the door of the study room, several of the Prince's servants had seen what happened. With beautiful music resounding through the palace, and joyous celebration taking place everywhere, why had the Prince been treated this way? As the Prince walked out followed by the Acharya, everyone could see the marks on his back. But no one questioned the Acharya as to why the Prince was punished.

Although the Prince walked directly back to his dressing room, the servants took a circuitous route. Word of the Acharya's punishment quickly spread. By the time the Prince was properly clothed and ornamented, the large assembly gathered knew of the incident. Everyone felt there must be a reason for the Acharya's action, but none could arrive at a satisfactory explanation.

The coronation ceremony was conducted, and it was the Acharya who joyously pronounced the former prince a King. Sitting back down, the Acharya found himself seated next to the kingdom's chief judge. Unable to restrain himself, the Judge said, "Mahatma, why did you punish your disciple?"

The Acharya's response was simple: "I saw the need for it." Having a great legal mind, the judge was not satisfied. "Does this mean the Prince did something wrong? Who and how did he offend?"

As the Acharya said, "Your Honor, he has done nothing whatsoever wrong," the Judge pressed his argument. "If for no reason, then why did you punish him? It seems unfair and undeserved."

The Acharya did not counter the Judge's argument but simply said, "The punishment itself was a teaching." The Judge was shaking his head and about to speak again when the newly crowned King appeared to be formally received by the Judge and Acharya.

Addressing his former student, the Acharya softly said, "My son, you were born in a king's family and raised with great love. Never have you disappointed me or anyone. But neither have you ever experienced physical punishment.

Since you have become King, it is necessary for you to not punish anyone without understanding how it feels yourself. It was thus my duty to provide a final lesson to you this morning. Whenever you punish someone in the future, you will remember this day and never give more punishment than is necessary."

Hearing these words, the Judge stood up only to fall prostrate at the Acharya's feet, saying "Mahatma, I am in awe of the art of your teaching. I promise you and the new King that I will never be unfair to anyone ever again."

The new King served for many years in this happy kingdom, carrying on the rule of a righteous line and well-served by a just judge.

Commentary

The role of a teacher is to further the highest welfare of the student. No matter how devoted the student, a teacher will be required to confront, challenge, and otherwise catalyze needed change. The irony of this story is that punishment is required only because of the student's spotless history of right action.

The Acharya's personal virtue and mastery in the dharma of ruling a kingdom, something akin to leadership ethics today, make him held in high regard by everyone in the palace. Even when the Acharya appears to act cruelly, they suspend judgment and do not jump to wrong conclusions. This trust is most evident in the Prince, who models the qualities of a good student.

As the story unfolds, it becomes clear that the Acharya's purpose is not just schooling the Prince, but rather instilling the qualities that ensure he will be a wise, compassionate, and righteous ruler. Seen thus, the Acharya's loyalty is not just to the royal family but to all the citizens of the land.

This deeper purpose of the Acharya also manifests through the surprising turn of events that produces a change of heart in the Judge. Such is the magic of an Acharya.

It is noteworthy that the King's coronation ceremony, which is outwardly a celebration of his power and glory, entails an inward humbling. Leadership is not a means to meet egocentric needs, but answering a call to public service.

History

Yoga recognizes a spectrum of teachers. A *pandit* is a scholar who conveys academic or theoretical knowledge. An *acharya* is an adept teacher in any area of learning who transmits life mastery. The syllable *gu* means darkness and *ru* means light. Thus the title *guru* implies the capacity to dispel a student's inner darkness by guiding him or her along a spiritual path that leads into the light of conscious awareness.

Chapter Eight

Greatness in Students

Teachers are complemented by *students*, individuals thirsty for knowledge and actively engaged in a conscious process of self-development. A great student is humble, open to receive the contribution of others and respectful of the wisdom earned by countless individuals in the past. A great student is also discriminating, digesting whatever is offered by actively questioning and testing it.

The yoga tradition placed great emphasis on becoming a fit and deserving student. Not infrequently, aspirants would have to serve a teacher for years before being accepted for instruction. To Swami Kripalu, being a student was a state of mind and heart that facilitated learning. Its essence was humility, which emptied the head of proud notions. Trust in the teacher was also essential, as it bestowed confidence in the lessons being taught.

The next story involves an unparalleled student famous throughout the yoga tradition.

Eklavya, Student of Archery

Maharishi Dronacharya, was a great and powerful master. As a teacher of archery, he was famous the world over. Kings and princes would come from great distances to sit at his feet and learn the science of archery. Among many other students, Dronacharya was the guru of the five Pandava princes.

Eklavya, the son of Nishadraj Hiranyadhanu, had a great love for archery and heard about the fame of Dronacharya.

Eklavya's mother, not wanting his sons feelings to be hurt, told him that Dronacharya would never accept him as a disciple. As a Shudra or person from the lowest caste, it was futile to dream of such privileges. Still, with much enthusiasm, Eklavya went to Hastinapura and sought out the ashram of Dronacharya.

Surrounded by a crowd of disciples, Dronacharya was returning to his residence after completing his teaching for the day. Eklavya recognized Dronacharya immediately and bowed down with love.

Dronacharya asked, "Whose son are you and why have you come?" He responded, "I am Eklavya, the son of Nishadraj Hiranyadhanu, and I have come to learn the science of archery from you."

Dronacharya gazed at Eklavya without blinking. Eklavya was standing there humbly and respectfully, with his hands folded, asking by gesture to be accepted as a student. Dronacharya looked around at the surrounding crowd of kings and princes. Suddenly, for just a second, there was a sign of grief on his face, but no one noticed it.

Although Eklavya was a Shudra by birth, Dronacharya could see he was in fact a prince. At that time, Kshatriya princes were considered superior. They never let Shudras study with them. Eklavya's request to become an archery student caused the ears of all the princes to perk up, as they wanted to hear Dronacharya's reply.

With great affection, Dronacharya said, "Son, as a river full of water never disappoints a thirsty man, an acharya who is full of knowledge never wants to disappoint an eager student. While I am an acharya, I am not free. I am bound to serve only

Kshatriya princes, because I am paid to do so by their kingly fathers. Due to the caste system, I cannot teach you."

Sometimes social custom imposes impenetrable restrictions, even for great masters. The Kshatriya princes were satisfied with Dronacharya's response.

There was a terrible pain of anguish on the shy face of Eklavya, who was very eager to learn archery. His mental suffering touched the heart of Dronacharya and at once there was a flow of compassion between the two. Dronacharya continued, "My son, I bless you. May you become the best archer."

New inspiration suddenly came to Eklavya, exhilarating his whole body. The expression on his face changed to one of ecstasy and humble joy. Eklavya bowed low and touched Dronacharya's feet. With tears in his eyes, he expressed his gratitude. "Gurudev, may you always be victorious. Today you have bestowed upon me the highest grace. Your infallible blessing is my wealth. The archers of the entire world will be jealous of what you have given me today."

The princes did not like this last sentence of Eklavya, thinking him conceited and whimsical. Dronacharya, however, understood Eklavya's inner process and took him seriously. In that moment, he saw unusual genius in Eklavya, who had the heart of a true disciple and received his guru's blessings as the boon of God.

Eklavya left Hastinapura with infinite enthusiasm and joy. After finding a secluded spot in the woods, he worked day and night to make a clay idol of his beloved Gurudev. The image of his guru poured out from his memory, mind, intellect, eyes, and fingers and was faithfully reproduced in the clay.

Eklavya made another Dronacharya, and there was no thought in any corner of his mind that it was merely an idol of clay. By making an idol of his guru, he became one with his guru.

After installing the idol of his gurudev, Eklavya began his study of archery. He slept very little and ate sparingly. Each morning he arose early. After finishing his routines, he would pick flowers and present them to the idol. He would bow down, pray, and bow again. Then drawing on the presence of his guru, he would ask "Gurudev, how should I begin my study of archery today?" As he felt his guru's presence, an answer would come from his inner conscience and he would respond accordingly. Time passed with Eklavya lost in his study and practice.

One day, the Pandava princes went to the forest to hunt wild game. The royal servants were walking behind the chariots carrying the things necessary for the hunt. The entourage included a hunting dog who strayed near the spot where Eklavya was practicing. On seeing his dark skin, and the way he wore his hair piled on the top of his head, the dog began to bark loudly. Not liking this interruption of his studies, Eklavya shot seven arrows into the mouth of the dog to silence him. Though otherwise uninjured, the dog was frightened and ran back to his masters.

Arjuna, the best archer among all the princes, was the first to see the dog. Astonished, he called to his brothers and said, "Come and look. Imagine the quickness and accuracy of the archer who could silence the sound of a barking dog by filling his mouth with arrows. His skill far surpasses that of mine. That brave archer who did this must be in the vicinity, so let us search for him."

Arjuna and his brothers began to search the forest and soon came to the place where Eklavya was practicing. Although they had all seen him before, no one recognized him because his appearance was totally different. Arjuna was the first to speak, "May I have your introduction please."

He replied, "My name is Eklavya. I am a disciple of Dronacharya." After freely praising Eklavya's skill, effort, and love for archery, the princes left. Returning to the city, they recounted the whole story to their guru. Although the other princes left to go home, Arjuna remained standing beside his guru with a shy expression on his face.

Dronacharya understood his reason for standing, and yet he said, "My son, do you want to ask me something?"

Arjuna collapsed on the ground. Holding his guru's feet, he started crying. After a few moments Arjuna was able to express his feelings, "Guruji, you have given me a blessing. Embracing me to your heart, you said that you would make me the best archer among all your disciples. How is it that Eklavya is more talented than me?"

Dronacharya remained silent for a few moments. Taking his disciples two hands, Dronacharya raised Arjuna up and embraced him. "Come, take me to the place where Eklavya is practicing."

Arjuna walked ahead, and Dronacharya followed him. As they drew near, the sound of the bowstring became very clear. When Eklavya saw his guru in the distance, he happily hurried toward him. Bowing low, a river of tears flowed from his eyes. Sobbing, he said "Gurudev, why have you pained your holy feet to give me your audience?"

Upon seeing such devotion, the eyes of Dronacharya and Arjuna also filled with tears. Dronacharya thought to himself, "Although Eklavya is a Shudra in this birth, it is possible that he was a Brahman, Kshatriya or a Vaishya in a past lifetime. Although he has outstanding qualities, he is still a Shudra nonetheless and must be regarded as such."

Eklavya brought them to his hut, and Dronacharya saw his image. Aware of the devotion of this disciple for his guru, love flowed from his heart toward Eklavya. Eklavya worshiped his guru according to the tradition, and bowed down before Dronacharya, who said, "My son, be blessed."

After remaining silent for a time, Dronacharya asked, "Do you believe that I am your guru?" Eklavya said, "Yes." Dronacharya continued, "Then it is time to give me your guru dakshina (gift.)"

Hearing his guru's words, Eklavya was overwhelmed. "Gurudev, what can I sacrifice. Be gracious and give me your command. There is nothing I will not give to you."

"Cut off the thumb of your right hand and offer it to me as your guru gift," instructed Dronacharya. The atmosphere became very still, and even the leaves on the trees stopped moving. Arjuna was stunned to hear the demand of his guru. To ask for the thumb of an archer was equivalent to killing him.

Yet hearing this order, Eklavya felt no hesitation or turmoil. With an expression of joy on his face, he cut off his thumb and placed it at his guru's feet. Witnessing this act, Arjuna felt small and stunted. There was no doubt that his guru brother was far superior in knowledge, skill, and devotion. But Arjuna's position as top archer was now secure.

Eklavya quickly stopped the flow of blood by bandaging the wound. Dronacharya asked, "Son, has this command caused you any pain?"

Eklavya was silent for a moment as he decided whether or not to speak his mind. Then he said, "Guruji, I will only speak the truth in your presence. I have experienced infinite suffering. I offered my entire body to you, and you only asked for the thumb from my right hand. By severing my thumb, I have not offered you a true gift. You have given me my whole life, and I have given back only a minute portion of it. Upon your command, I will deposit the rest of my body at your holy feet."

Dronacharya stood up, embraced Eklavya and lovingly patted his head.

Eklavya continued, "Gurudev, you are very generous. In return for an ordinary thumb, you have given me so much, so much that I have difficulty in accepting it. You are omniscient and a great warrior as well. You know everything. Why do you attach so much importance to my ordinary thumb? It easily could have been severed by the sharp arrow of an enemy."

Before he left, Dronacharya demonstrated to Eklavya a way to grasp the arrow and draw the bowstring using his middle fingers and pinkie. After this incident, Eklavya continued to practice daily, but he was not able to shoot as fast.

Swami Kripalu's Commentary

The story of Eklavya was presented as part of a formal discourse on idol worship. During and after its telling, Swami Kripalu made the following remarks to clarify the story:

In this story, Eklavya's infinite faith in his guru brings the inanimate idol alive. Eklavya's devotion towards the idol allows him to enter a stage of meditation beyond the senses where one can one attain supreme knowledge. Through his love, Eklavya feels his guru's presence and is skillfully instructed in the science of archery.

To understand how this could be, let us look at today's psychologists who have also conducted surprising experiments. A hypnotist can place a piece of ice in a subject's hand and suggest that it is a burning coal. Instantly, the subject throws away what is believed to be a burning coal and a blister becomes visible in his palm. This blister is also the result of a steady faith.

Eklavya was receiving inspiration from within, yet his experience was that he was being told what to do by the idol. Due to the firmness of his faith, he became a yogi open to the suggestion of the divine. His idol worship was not ignorance; it was meditation and the science of yoga.

Saints are the well wishers of all. Since they wish the best for everyone, they often say so. But there is a difference between best wishes and a blessing. Saints silently and spontaneously bestow an energetic blessing (*shaktipat*) upon the deserving. A saint full of sympathy will sometimes bestow a blessing upon an undeserving person. However, the blessing cannot be fully realized until the person becomes deserving. Sooner or later, the person matures and the intended benefit comes to pass. Thus it can be said that the blessing of a saint never fails.

Having received Dronacharya's blessing, Eklavya is able to behold his guru with love, even after he is asked to cut off his thumb. If one looks at another through the window of his virtues, he sees the most ordinary person as great. If he looks at another through the window of his vices, even the greatest person is made ordinary in his sight. By viewing others in the light of their virtues, there is love instead of hatred.

Did Dronacharya do an injustice to Eklavya? No, when one is about to receive a blow to his head, he stops it with his hand. When a hand suffers a blow on behalf of the head, it is not dishonored. The status of the hand actually increases. In order to protect his guru's virtue, Eklavya sacrifices his thumb and prowess. In willingly doing so, he retains his faith and devotion as a disciple. This is of paramount importance to Eklavya as a yogi because liberation is always dependent on the ability to receive grace.

Commentary

While told to illustrate the power of idol worship, this story is also a teaching on the student/teacher relationship. As EKlavya's experience makes clear, a student's faith and trust are foremost factors in creating a psychological environment in which depth learning and transformation can occur. When faith is firm and trust lends confidence to action, miraculous results can occur with minimal involvement of the guru.

Looked at more deeply, Eklavya's story is a profound depiction of the process of spiritual awakening. Like everyone, Eklavya embarks on the path based on "the myth of enlightenment." Idealistic, enthusiastic, and sincere, Eklavya believes that through disciplined efforts he will become the best archer in the world and find fulfillment in life.

During the first phase of the path, Eklavya engages fully in his practice, gains amazing prowess, and to some extent manifests his dreams. Swami Kripalu called this part of the path "privritti dharma" which means "the path with mind," what Kripalu

Yoga calls "willful practice."

Through mental focus and disciplined action, a seeker can attain three of what yoga calls "the four nobles aims of life." These three are prosperity, comfort, and the virtuous character that brings self-esteem and the respect of your peers. Swami Kripalu praised privritti dharma and its stated goal of success in life, encouraging householders disciples to "establish yourself like a sun in the solar system of society."

Swami Kripalu was also clear that the fourth aim of life, moksha or spiritual freedom, required "nivritti dharma" or "the path without mind." Because we embark on the spiritual path with an egocentric mindset, we naturally expect that enlightenment will be a crowning event, like the coronation ceremony of our last story. Yet the "truth of enlightenment" always involves a humbling. Ultimately, nothing will suffice except the surrender of the personal self, and all its stories of fulfillment in the future, into the white hot fire of pure being that is the impersonal or transpersonal Self.

Eklavya is a student of the highest caliber, and everything changes as his path shifts to surrender. Eklavya's right thumb represents his ego. Through willful disciplines, Eklavya has honed his skills to the utmost, but neither proficiency nor success is the ultimate goal of yoga. His guru, Dronacharya, represents God. Dronacharya's status and good standing, symbolized by his promise to make Arjuna the best disciple, represents the good of the whole. Surrendering completely, Eklavya sacrifices everything he has gained. Nothing less is sufficient if a student is to know freedom.

After losing his thumb, Eklavya goes back to his practice. It is easy to imagine the rest of his story. While losing his position as the world's best archer, he spiritually attains to the highest.

History

Arjuna grows up to become a great warrior and play a major role in the Mahabharat. As a close devotee of Krishna and the best archer in the world, circumstances unfold in which Arjuna must kill Dronacharya, his beloved guru. Krishna's instructions to Arjuna on the battlefield of Kurukshetra comprise the Bhagavad Gita.

Chapter Nine

Let the Seeker Beware

Even among yoga enthusiasts, the terms "guru" and "disciple" elicit a mixed response, and understandably so. Where the teachings of every yoga school emphasize the need to study under a competent spiritual master, the scandalous abuses of contemporary Eastern and Western gurus have cast doubt upon the whole notion of spiritual authority and discipleship.

Traditionally, disciples came to gurus to enter into a unique relationship. They were seeking initiation into an esoteric tradition, aware that it had a distinct set of teachings and practices, and at least marginally conscious of the rigorous journey they were undertaking.

In India, the guru/disciple relationship was surrounded by a set of cultural ideals that encouraged clarity of purpose and mutual trust. The guru's role was to skillfully and selflessly guide the disciple's development. Disciples were to focus their lives on their study and practice, adopt a reverent attitude, ask questions with humility, and follow the guru's guidance without doubt or hesitation.

Even in India, cultural ideals have never been guarantees that individuals will act accordingly. As unquestioned authorities, self-serving gurus can manipulate disciples for personal gain and aggrandizement. Disciples seeking to avoid the difficult inner work of individuation can place their guru on a pedestal and foster dependency instead of courageously taking responsibility for their own spiritual journey.

Swami Kripalu considered it essential for disciples to remain discerning and discriminating. Just because something is ancient, venerated by others, or praised by a popular teacher does not make it right for you. Close scrutiny of your own experience is the only means by which real learning occurs. This is the story of what can happen if an aspirant is bereft of those essential qualities.

The Guru With No Nose

Once there was a dimwitted devotee named Augar Bhagat. The leader of a chanting group, Augar used to cry profusely while singing the name of the Lord. Convinced his longing for the divine was profound, Augar was held in high esteem by his audiences. In truth, Augar had just discovered that people were more interested in his crying than his singing. Relaxing the muscles of his face, and letting his tear glands open wide, it appeared that Augar was crying out to God as his last resort, but it was only a way of winning over people.

One evening Augar attended a discourse by a popular spiritual teacher. Traveling from town to town, this teacher's manner was so creative and enchanting that everyone would shutter their shops or stop whatever they were doing to come and listen. Drawing his talk to a masterful close, the audience was spellbound as the teacher said, "Lovers of God, the Lord who also loves his devotees is not far from you. In fact, he is very close." These words pierced directly into Augar Bhagat's heart, who murmured to himself, "Oh, Augar, you are a devotee and yet you are so blind. While the Lord is near at hand, you are not able to see him."

Now listening intently, Augar's mind became steady and he was eager to hear what was next. The teacher continued, "There is one reason why you don't see the Lord. And that is your useless nose." He continued, "Lovers of God, unless and until we cut off this nose it will be impossible to see the Lord."

Augar thought to himself, "Just because of this useless nose, I cannot see the Lord? Why so much attachment to the nose, which I can live without? But I cannot live without the Lord any longer." In that moment, Augar Bhagat firmly decided, "Tomorrow I will cut off this nose, which is coming between me and the Lord."

The teacher came to his concluding remark, "My friends, the nose that I'm talking about is not the nose that takes breath in and out. The nose of which I speak is the ego. The devotee who cuts off this nose of ego can truly see the Lord." Sadly, none of these words entered the ears of Augar Bhagat. Certain he had already churned the essence of this lecture into butter, Augar had stopped listening and begun planning.

The crowd dispersed and Augar walked home to prepare for the morning. Next day, he got up very early. Finishing his morning routines, Augar entered his meditation room and lay prone in front of his altar. Uttering prayers, he lit the ghee lamp and performed puja to his picture of the Lord. At the end, he prayed again.

Then Augar took a knife with a very sharp edge in his hand. For a few minutes, he gazed at the picture. Then with great faith, he swiftly cut his nose off. The blood flowed freely, yet Augar wasn't the least bit shaken. He opened his eyes wide and waited, thinking, "Now my Lord will definitely appear in front of me."

After five minutes had passed, Augar put a bandage on his nose. A few hours passed and the bleeding gradually stopped. Then the day passed, and the night passed. Three days passed this way, and he still had not seen the Lord. Augar was feeling that the scriptures are nothing but lies, that spiritual teachers are cunning liars, and that God doesn't exist. Almost wanting to murder that lecturer, he thought, "How will I be able to live in this society, without a nose? Along with the nose went all my status and respect." Afraid to go outside, Augar did not know what to do.

Augar's neighbor noticed what was going on and said to his freinds, "Augar has been in his meditation room for three days, without coming out at all." The neighborhood gathered and called to him, with no answer. They called more loudly and then shouted at the top of their lungs. The devotee without the nose didn't answer or open the door at all.

Finally the men began taking off Augar's door. As they pulled the door from its hinges, they saw Augar Bhagat dancing and singing with a very funny nasally sound: "Bhajo Radhe Govinda, Bhajo Radhe Govinda." He had firmly decided not to look at anyone else and appeared completely engrossed. The sound of the Lord's name was coming from where Augar's nose had been, and there on the altar was the bloody nose, in front of the picture. Seeing this, the mystery was quickly solved: the devotee Augar Bhagat had cut off his nose and offered it to the Lord.

One fellow took hold of Augar to stop him from dancing. He acted as if coming out of deep meditation and feigned great surprise when he looked at everybody. Then he started bowing down to everybody, as if he was just coming from the other shore. At the same time, he started crying. Only the crying was genuine, for he did not want anyone to see him without his nose. The thought, "What will happen to my name and fame?" was so painful that he naturally cried.

Another fellow said, "Devotee Augar, what are you doing? What has happened to you?" Augar did not answer. Neither did he stop bowing or crying. He just went on as if crazy with God intoxication. When everyone repeated the questions loudly, Augar said, "Brothers and sisters, how can I describe it to you? It is something beyond words. I have found my Lord. My life is complete. Here, I see him right here. What a beautiful headdress! What a beautiful, lovely face! My Lord, I am totally fulfilled."

All his neighbors were looking at him with their eyes wide open. They completely believed what Augar was saying. Several tripped over each other, trying to bow down at Augar's feet. Augar was pleased and started ruminating, "If I lost my nose but become very famous, that won't be too bad."

As Augar refused to let people bow down to him, others became crazy to bow at his holy feet. Within a short time, the whole town had come and bowed. This had an immediate effect on all the surrounding towns and villages. The message quickly spread: "Augar Bhagat has seen the Lord personally." Soon crowds came every day to receive the darshan of this great devotee.

Stories of all kinds of miracles started spreading. Somebody said, "This king of devotees created food through his mantra power to feed the poor." Another said, "Hundreds of poor souls received bags of money from this devotee's power and grace." Still another related that, "Blessed Augarji healed me of my lifelong malady."

In only one week, the devotee became God himself. He was offered silk clothes to wear, silver sandals to walk upon, and velvet cushions on which to sit. He ate with utensils of gold while wealthy people fanned him. There was no end to Augar's prosperity.

And yet, Augar Bhagat continued to think to himself, "While I got many things, I still lost my nose. All these people have noses, and I do not."

Augar started giving spiritual discourses, saying, "Lovers of God, the God who loves his devotees is not far from us. In fact, he is very close. The only thing between you and the Lord is your nose. If you cut off that nose, you will instantly see the Lord. The procedure and technique will be shown only to one who receives initiation from me."

Because Shri Augar Bhagat was speaking through his own noseless face, it was a very moving lecture. Hundreds of devotees were inspired to be initiated. On their initiation morning, everybody worshipped their guru with great faith and offered their guru gifts. Then, according to the guidance of the guru, and with a sharp knife, each disciple cut off his own nose, and offered it to the Lord's feet. Immediately, the ceremony of the bandage was performed.

While the devotees were still on fire with desire to see the Lord, Augar Bhagat gave his most impressive lecture, "Listen to me. I haven't found the Lord by cutting the nose, and you're not going to find him either. There is no animal like God anywhere on this earth. Even if you search for a thousand years, sacrificing not only your nose but also your head, you're still not going to find him."

"This is the knowledge of Brahman I received by cutting my nose. I have absolutely no doubt about what I am telling you. That is why, looking after your welfare, I have given you this knowledge. If you are now to say that you haven't seen the Lord, other people will know that you are foolish. As long as you live, people will insult you by calling you 'the one without the nose.'"

"My beloved disciples, in order to live happily from now on, tell everyone, "We see the Lord right here." Just by saying this, you will be greatly respected in society. You won't have to suffer any damages. This is the secret knowledge of our path. And this is to be guarded with great care, and given only to a faithful disciple, after he cuts his nose, and not before that."

The disciples were very angry with their guru, and almost wanted to kill him. This was true to their tradition, as Augar Bhagat had felt similarly. But they thought, "Now that the nose is cut, it is not going to grow again. Killing him will bring us only more pain and suffering. The way he has shown is our best chance at happiness."

So the disciples came out to meet the public, who were eager to see the results. All those without noses began singing, "Bhajo Radhe Govinda" and dancing. A few shared their experience, "There is no end to the bliss. The Lord Himself, by His grace, has given us His darshan. This life is now complete." Then everybody started singing, "Bhajo Radhe Govinda."

Hundreds of devotees came from all directions to receive initiation. Within only six months, the following of this guru became extremely large. Inspired devotees composed bhajans and poetry, whose essence was, "Our guru, Augar himself, is the incarnation of the Lord. All our pains have left us through the grace of his teaching. He alone has found the true path of yoga, one which is unparalleled on this whole earth. The scriptures say that prana must enter the shushumna nadi. The left nostril is called the ida nadi. The right is the pingala. When the flow of both meet in the center, that flow is called shushumna nadi. By cutting the nose, this shushumna opens, and the ajna chakra suddenly blossoms."

Augar became "Augar Maharaj" and was constantly in the company of powerful men and kings. Surrounded by hundreds and then thousands of noseless devotees, Augar ceased feeling any pain around the loss of his own nose. Even the king respected Augar Maharaj highly, and he was given a special residence in the palace, where other kings, queens and princes could easily have his darhsan. The sun of Augar Bhagat's fame was now fully shining and he said to everyone, "I have dedicated my entire life to spread this knowledge of Brahman."

Soon the king himself was ready to take initiation. He spoke to his chief minister, who was a very intelligent and insightful man. The minister said, "My beloved King, I don't see much of value in this talk about cutting the nose to see the Lord. I think you should remain cautious, aware, and alert."

Just yesterday, the king had been impressed with Augar's explanation of the yogic scriptures: "Rishis from the ancient times have said that the Lord resides in shushumna itself. When the nose is cut, He cannot remain secret and has to appear in front of the devotee." The minister said, "What Augar Maharaj is saying may be supported by the scriptures, and hundreds of devotees are being initiated by him every day, but let me inquire in a secret way. Only if I find it proper will you take initiation."

Persuaded by his Minister's counsel, both the king and the minister hid themselves in the initiation room. They saw the ceremony, and heard the detailed discourse of this Augar Maharaj. The king could not control his anger. He ordered the immediate execution of Augar Bhagat and revealed his pretense to the world. All his former devotees admitted their mistake, saying, "We were cheated by this cunning teacher. Not one among us has seen the Lord." Thus the path of noseless people stopped suddenly.

In this world of pretense, a sincere seeker is often troubled, tested, and taken advantage of. Whenever someone deceives you, it is easy to think you are losing something. Remember that you also receive knowledge in the process of being disillusioned. In a similar way, mistakes committed in ignorance may hurt tremendously, but without mistakes and bad experiences you cannot come to right knowledge. Where the inspiration received in books and discourses is usually placed in the storehouse of memory where it cannot help you, the knowledge received from your own difficulties in life becomes immediately useful. Thus it can be said that even the dimwitted devotee Augar Bhagat was being of service.

Commentary

When read closely, this macabre tale offers a scathing critique of popular Indian spirituality. Devotees lacking discernment bestow godhood onto teachers of modest attainment and questionable character. Deceitful gurus take advantage of sincere but naïve seekers. The end result for both is not pretty or positive.

This story suggests that one should be suspect of any teacher who asks you to disfigure yourself on any level. This is not to imply that the spiritual path does not require self sacrifice, which it certainly does. Yet what is ruthlessly cut away is our false conceptions of who we are. The only thing we lose is what we are not.

Swami Kripalu spoke out against gurus who encourage seekers to engage in extreme practices like holding an arm aloft until joint mobility is lost and the limb withers, which he felt produced little if any good. In *Premyatra, Pilgrimage of Love,* Swami Kripalu taught that "Tapas should be performed only with the intention of purifying mind and body. One who practices tapas to gain honor, respect, or reverence is misguided and their tapas is usually short-lived. Others perform austerities in a foolish, obstinate, or compulsive way. Although they may gain some determination, the body remains impure and the mind unsteady. In the long run, this kind of tapasvin only tortures and causes injury to himself."

"Seekers should bear in mind that these kinds of tapas have been practiced for thousands of years. Whole lineages exist, and their gurus attract large followings. Yet the wise do not give these types of austerities much importance, since they are performed without discrimination."

Serving in the role of a spiritual teacher is not easy, and success like that enjoyed by Augar Bhagat brings even more difficulties. In the words of Swami Kripalu, "In the beginning, a devotee's aim is the realization of the highest. When many people are attracted to him because of his disciplines, love of God, and good conduct, most devotees lose their guiding purpose. Mass popularity leads them astray. By attaining the status of a master, they forever lose their status as a student. When this occurs, the inevitable result is the downfall of the devotee."

History

The source of this cautionary tale is unknown and let's hope entirely fictional. Swami Kripalu ended this discourse by saying, "It is not possible for me to tell you this story as a dharmacharya (spiritual teacher). Only as a grandfather, is it proper for me to speak through my nose such." Then he began the chant "Radhe Govinda Bhajo."

Chapter Ten

Keeping the Faith

The scriptures of yoga stress that faith or *astikya* is an invisible component of any spiritual practice. Swami Kripalu made this point by saying, "It is according to the degree of faith that one has in *devas* (celestial beings), *tirthas* (pilgrimage places), the blessings of saints, *mantras* (holy words), sacred teachings, the predictions of astrologers, and the guru's guidance that one attains to accomplishment."

This is a story of what can happen when prayer is empowered by a pure and child-like faith.

The Umbrella

Once upon a time, there was a small village suffering from a severe drought. Not a drop of rain had fallen for three years. Although various methods were employed to produce rain, nothing had worked, and the inhabitants were hungry, thirsty, and disheartened.

With all else having failed, everyone's attention was drawn toward a last resort: praying to the Lord. The villagers, acting mainly from a sense of utter helplessness, decided to hold a public prayer meeting.

As the meeting time drew near, a crowd began to congregate at the appointed spot. A few musicians began to sing a bhajan, and soon the whole group was chanting in call and response. Some distance away, a ten year-old orphan boy named Chapalkumar entered the humble house of his poor grandmother who had cared for him since he was seven.

96

"Grandmother," he said, "I want to go and pray for rain. Where is my umbrella?"

"Umbrella?" she replied quizzically. "Yes," said Chapalkumar. It's been a very long time since it has rained, and I've forgotten where I placed it.

"Go look in the corner near the cupboard," said his grandmother. Chapalkumar did as he was told and found his umbrella. "Did you find it?" she asked. "Yes," he confirmed, running quickly out the door to the site of the prayer meeting.

Entering the street, Chapalkumar saw many men and women headed in the same direction. Satisfied he was not late, he began walking along with the crowd. Everyone who saw the umbrella under his arm smiled. Many whispered among themselves, "For the last three years our unfortunate land has not had a single drop of rain, and there is not a sign of rain in sight anywhere, yet this boy is carrying an umbrella!"

A neighbor asked, "Hey Chapal, why are you carrying an umbrella?" The boy replied sincerely, as if he were correcting the man's attitude, "Why shouldn't I bring my umbrella? We are all going to pray to the Lord, so He will, of course, be sending rain, and we will all get wet." Touched by the lad's faith and somewhat abashed, the man replied, "Why of course! Yes, you are right, young man. Why, I ran out of the house in such a hurry that I forgot my umbrella."

People around them were listening to the conversation, and someone called out to the gentleman: "Brother, why are you worried? Don't we have Chapalkumar's umbrella? If it rains, we can all take shelter under it. Chapal, will you allow us to share your umbrella?"

97

Chapal, quite delighted, said, "Yes, but how can we all fit under this small umbrella?" "Don't worry about it," someone said. "We will find a way."

Soon, everyone was gathered for prayer and the chanting stopped. A well-known village elder stood up. In sorrowful tones, he described the havoc wrought by the drought. Then, after praising the greatness of God, he expounded on the power of prayer. Concluding with the humble plea, he directed the group, "Dearest brothers and sisters, let us pray silently to the compassionate Lord with pure hearts for just two minutes."

He then began praying, "Oh Compassionate One, bring us rain! On Compassionate One, bring us rain! Oh, Compassionate One, bring us rain!"

No one believed that the prayers would really bring rain, but no sooner had they begun their heartfelt prayer when a sudden flash of lightning crackled across the sky. It was followed immediately by a loud clap of thunder, and the wind suddenly picked up and began to blow fiercely.

Within moments, the sky was filled with dense clouds, and everyone's eyes were filled with tears. It was as if the prayers had come to life. Another bhajan was started, and everyone heartily joined in. Soon the rain was pouring down in torrents, and everyone started to leave.

Chapalkumar's joy could not be contained, and he was dancing ecstatically. Opening his umbrella, he invited everyone to join him under it. "Come! Come! Come enjoy the shelter of my umbrella!" A man hoisted Chapalkumar onto his shoulders, and the entire crowd began to walk as if each person were covered by the umbrella.

Quenched by the rains, no one asked what power had worked this miracle. Was Chapalkumar's umbrella then just an umbrella? No, it was an affirmation of faith in the Lord's grace.

Commentary

The realm of faith is not limited to religion or worship. All actions are motivated by a faith that they will produce desirable and worthwhile results. Similarly, all actions that are abandoned are given up because of a lack of faith. Looked at in this light, it can be said that faith is the seed of any accomplishment.

Although written thousands of years ago, the *Bhagavad Gita* describes the importance of this kind of faith in contemporary psychological terms. The minds of most people are fickle and agitated. Due to unclarity and unsteadiness, they cannot make a firm decision. Due to lack of a firm decision, they cannot act dynamically and sustain actions over time. Because of this, their efforts fail and they cannot achieve lasting happiness.

Swami Kripalu believed that actively cultivating faith was the best way to turn this vicious circle around. Faith is never defeated by failure. If faith does not succeed with one action, it tries another, and after that a third.

Instead of growing discouraged and despondent, a person of strong faith becomes increasingly awake, aware, and alive when facing adversity. This is important, as so many endeavors in life do not bear fruit quickly. They must be pursued patiently for many years to truly discover if one's faith is warranted. One such endeavor is self-transformation through yoga.

Distilled to its essence, the *Bhagavad Gita* describes two paths. The first is the path of renunciation of action. The second is the path of "holy action" or karma yoga. Both paths are described as having an enemy that a practitioner must slay to successfully see the journey through to completion.

The enemy on the path of renunciation is desire, which agitates the mind and leads to unconscious, habitual, and often harmful actions. The enemy on the path of karma yoga is doubt, which prevents one from trusting in one's self and acting confidently based on inner knowing.

These traditional paths roughly correspond to the two phases of Kripalu Yoga. Willful practice is a process of renouncing your habitual ways of being. This is done by using a variety of spiritual practices to overcome inertia and shift out of the well-worn ruts of self-limiting patterns. To actually do this, a practitioner will have to do battle with the enemy of desire. Its many guises include laziness, distraction, and apathy. Discipline is the antidote to this kind of desire, empowered by a faith in one's chosen practices.

Surrender is a process of attuning to Self and letting actions flow from a place of deep connection to the whole. In surrendered action, "you," the small and limited self, are not the doer. As actions flow, both on the yoga mat and in life, doubt will inevitably arise in the mind over whether they are the right ones. Faith is the antidote to this kind of doubt, empowered by a wisdom that grows from witnessing the results in your life of this kind of "inaction in action."

Brief Chronology of the Kripalu Tradition

Seven great seers establish Vedic culture,   3,500 BCE
those being Atri, Bharadvaja, Kashyapa,
Jamadagni, Gautama, Vashishtha and Vishvamitra.

Writing of Rig Veda that contains Gayatri   3,000 BCE
mantra. Cities of Harappa and Mahenjo-Daro
where clay "Pashupat Seal" is found bearing
likeness of Shiva.

Krishna and events narrated in Mahabharat   2,000 BCE
and Bhagavad Gita.

Lakulish establishes Pashupat religious order   200
and authors the Pashupat Sutra.

Islamic invaders destroy temples throughout   1000
central India. Legends say that idol of Lakuish
is buried by devotees to protect it.

Idol of Lakulish is found in farmers field   1866
just outside Kayavarohon, India.

Approximate birth date of Bankimbabu who   1870
becomes renouncate monk called "Pranavanda."

Birth of Swami Kripalu.   1913

Swami Kripalu meets his guru and lives in his   1932
guru's Bombay ashram for a year and a quarter.

Swami Kripalu becomes a renunciate member   1942
of the religious order of swamis.

Swami Kripalu jumps in Narmada river.   1954

Swami Kripalu invited to speak at Kayavarohan   1955
where he recognizes statue of Lakulish and begins
process of rebuilding Brahmaeshvar temple.

Founding of Philadelphia nonprofit organization   1966
by Yogi Amrit Desai and others that trains yoga
teachers and later becomes Kripalu Center
for Yoga & Health.

Brahmeshvar temple is completed.   1974
Philadelphia non-profit shifts emphasis
and relocates to Sumneytown PA where it
becomes "Kripalu Yoga Ashram." Quickly'
expands to second facility in Summit Station PA.

Swami Kripalu comes to America where he   1977
spends last four years of his life in seclusion and
intensive yoga practice at Sumneytown ashram,
where he teaches Yogi Amrit Desai and is
personally served by Mataji Urmilla Desai.

Swami Kripalu returns to India to die at 68.   1981
Kripalu Yoga evolves in residential community
of initiated disciples.

Residential community moves to present   1982
Kripalu Center facility in Lenox MA.

Yogi Amrit Desai resigns as Kripalu Center's   1994
guru and spiritual director.

Kripalu Center for Yoga & Health ceases being a   1995
"guru led" organization. Residential ashram
community begins to disband.

Kripalu reorganizes as a non-profit spiritual retreat   1998
and holistic program center based on yoga.

Kripalu Center establishes itself as a mainstream   2004
educational institution promoting the art and
science of yoga as the basis for a revitalized society.

About Kripalu Center

Imagine a place where you can escape daily stress, immerse yourself in the practice of yoga, and return home invigorated, energized and restored.

Kripalu Center is the largest retreat center for yoga and holistic living in North America, a distinction it has held for more than 25 years. Located in the beautiful Berkshire Mountains of western Massachusetts, Kripalu is a place to discover what it means to be fully human and fully alive through a non-dogmatic approach to yoga. Its renowned program curriculum is based on a model of experiential learning that provides people with tools for optimal living and a wealth of opportunities to cultivate vibrant physical health, nurture emotional wellness, and draw spiritual sustenance from within and without.

Kripalu's approach to yoga practice is unique, integrating the rigor of traditional yoga with advances in contemporary health science, growth psychology, and the work of today's pioneers in the study of consciousness. Kripalu Yoga empowers you to befriend and listen to your body, discovering from your own direct experience what practices support your well-being and growth. The tools of Kripalu Yoga awaken the life force yoga calls *prana.* This initiates a natural process of healing, growth, and transformation that reveals the vitality, goodness, and beauty that lies within each of us.

Kripalu Yoga is only one facet of what's happening at Kripalu Center. Swami Kripalu embraced the world's wisdom traditions, and in this same spirit Kripalu Center promotes all approaches that help people cultivate physical health, nurture emotional wellness, draw spiritual sustenance, and return home with tools that provide inspiration, energy, and integration. At Kripalu, we believe this non-sectarian *yoga of life* can do more than uplift us as individuals; it can serve as the foundation for a revitalized society and planet.

Kripalu is committed to making its services available to people from all backgrounds and social classes. Each year it provides full and partial scholarship assistance to hundreds of people each year attending various Kripalu Center programs. Scholarship applications can be obtained by e-mailing scholarship@kripalu.org.

History

In many ways, Kripalu's history parallels the evolution of yoga in America. In the late 1960s, Indian-born Amrit Desai taught yoga to a growing number of students in the Philadelphia area. In 1972, Yogi Desai and a handful of dedicated students established a small, residential yoga center in Sumneytown, Pennsylvania. It rapidly center expanded to nearby Summit Station, Pennsylvania, before moving to its current Lenox, Massachusetts, location in 1983.

From its inception, Kripalu Center was staffed by a committed group of yoga enthusiasts who formed the nucleus of an intentional yoga community or *ashram*. Yogi Desai was the ashram's spiritual leader, which eventually grew to offer a modest curriculum of yoga, holistic health, and self-discovery programs to the public. Developed and taught by ashram residents, these programs were the outgrowth of practices carried on within the community.

Yogi Desai's guru, Swami Kripalu, came to the United States in 1977 and spent the last four years of his life at the ashram. Although continuing his reclusive lifestyle of yoga practice,

Swami Kripalu's presence galvanized the growth of the ashram community and inspired thousands to join him in dedicated spiritual practice.

Kripalu Center continued to expand in size and influence until 1994. Yogi Desai was an international figure in yoga, and the ashram was considered an exemplary spiritual community with two Lenox facilities staffed by 325 hard-working residents. Even as he fell from his pedestal, Yogi Desai served as a catalyst for the evolution of the Kripalu community. The myth of the omnipotent guru was shattered, forcing the entire community to a higher level of individuation and self-empowerment.

With the bloom of the resident community fading, the ashram gradually disbanded. Kripalu Center restructured itself as an educational non-profit organization, hired its formerly volunteer staff, and broadened its program offerings. Kripalu has the distinction of being the first, and possibly the only, yoga center in North America to make a successful transition from a traditional guru-disciple structure.

Today Kripalu Center is much more than a program and retreat center. It is a university for the whole person, a place where everyone can experience the state of body, mind and spirit integration that is yoga and shift the consciousness from which we live our lives. At Kripalu, we believe that yoga and other contemplative practices have the potential to serve as the basis for a revitalized society.

For more information about Kripalu Center, its international network of more than two thousand yoga teachers, and a current catalog detailing hundreds of programs and retreats, visit www.kripalu.org. or call 800-741-7353

Myth or Substance

Shiva, Vishvamitra, Lakulish,
whether these figures exist in myth or
substance, I can't say which.

Who they are and what
they mean to me shifts
from day to day.

The stories of their transformations
point the way to the gateless gate,
the entryway to potent inner yoga.

Danna Faulds

About the Editor

A chance 1981 encounter with Swami Kripalu profoundly shifted the trajectory of Richard's life. Already a student of yoga, he embarked on a daily practice of yoga, pranayama, and meditation, and forged a close affiliation with Kripalu Center that continues today. As a Kripalu Center staff member, Richard has worn many hats: ashram resident, legal counsel, president, and senior teacher. Richard currently chairs Kripalu's Board of Trustees, and is best known in Kripalu circles by his Sanskrit name "Shobhan."

One of Richard's joys and missions in life is to practice the teachings of the Kripalu tradition deeply, and share them freely with others in contemporary terms. To serve that purpose, he earned a masters degree in Counseling and Human Development in 1996 which helped him integrate the views of East and West.

Richard has written *Kripalu Yoga: A Guide to Practice On and Off the Mat*, a comprehensive but easy to read book synthesizing the experience of the entire Kripalu community. He has also written a companion book to this volume called *Sayings of Swami Kripalu: Inspiring Quotes from a Contemporary Yoga Master*, along with numerous articles for Kripalu Center publications, many of which are posted on the KYTA page of Kripalu's website.

Richard live in the Shenandoah Valley of Virginia with his wife, poet Danna Faulds, where they practice yoga, tend a vegetable garden, and host individuals and small groups interested in the teachings of the Kripalu tradition. You can contact them by e-mail at yogapoems@aol.com.